Library of
Davidson College

JOHN T. WOOD is a staff member and group leader at Center for Studies of the Person, La Jolla, California. He is the author of *How Do You Feel? A Guide to Your Emotions.*

JOHN T. WOOD

What Are You Afraid Of?

A guide to
dealing with your fears

A SPECTRUM BOOK

Prentice-Hall, Inc., Englewood Cliffs, New Jersey

Library of Congress Cataloging in Publication Data

Wood, John (date).
  What are you afraid of?

  (A Spectrum Book)
  Includes bibliographical references and index.
  1. Fear. I. Title.
BF575.F2W57   152.4   75-31678
ISBN 0-13-951889-4
ISBN 0-13-951871-1 pbk.

© 1976 by Prentice-Hall, Inc., Englewood Cliffs, New Jersey. A SPECTRUM BOOK. All rights reserved. No part of this book may be reproduced in any form or by any means without permission in writing from the publisher. Printed in the United States of America.

10 9 8 7 6 5 4 3 2 1

Prentice-Hall International, Inc., *London*
Prentice-Hall of Australia Pty., Limited, *Sydney*
Prentice-Hall of Canada, Ltd., *Toronto*
Prentice-Hall of India Private Limited, *New Delhi*
Prentice-Hall of Japan, Inc., *Tokyo*
Prentice-Hall of Southeast Asia Private Limited, *Singapore*

To GREG *and* CHRIS *and their fears*

Contents

Introduction   xi

PART ONE: *Definitions of Fear*

    Chapter 1   WE ALL ARE AFRAID   3

    Chapter 2   FEAR IS . . .   21

    Chapter 3   ANXIETY AND PHOBIAS   32

    Chapter 4   FEAR AND OTHER EMOTIONS   46

PART TWO: *Responses to Fear*

Chapter 5   FEAR AND THE INDIVIDUAL   *59*

Chapter 6   FEAR BETWEEN US   *73*

Chapter 7   FEAR IN THE WORLD   *90*

PART THREE: *New Perspectives*

Chapter 8   FEAR AND DESIRE   *113*

Chapter 9   SEX, DEATH, AND SURRENDER   *122*

Chapter 10   WAYS OUT   *140*

Chapter 11   THE NEW   *158*

Index   175

It has been said that fear, which plays such a dominant role in our lives, was once a vague, nameless thing, an echo, one might almost say, of the life instinct. It has been said that with the development of civilization this nameless fear gradually crystallized into a fear of death. And that in the highest reaches of civilization this fear of death becomes a fear of life, as exemplified by the behavior of the neurotic. Now there is nothing strange about fear: no matter in what guise it preens itself it is something with which we are all so familiar that when a man appears who is without it we are at once enslaved by him. There have been less than a handful of such men in the history of man. Whether they were forces for good or evil matters little; the fear which they awaken is the fear of the monster. In truth they were all monsters, whether they be called Tamerlane, Buddha, Christ, or Napoleon. They were heroic figures, and the hero, according to myths, was always born supernaturally. The hero, in short, is one who was spared the shock of birth.

The hero then is a sort of monster who is immune to pain and suffering: he is on the side of life. The world is for him a place where things are engendered, brought to life. Life reveals itself to him as art, not as an ordeal. He enjoys life by rearranging it according to his own needs. He may say that he is doing it for others, for humanity, but we know that he is also a liar. The hero is a man who says to himself—this is where things happen, not somewhere else. He acts as if he were at home in the world. Such behavior, of course, brings about a terrific confusion, for as you may have noticed, people are seldom at home, always somewhere else, always "absent." Life, as it is called, is for most of us one long postponement. And the simple reason for it is: FEAR.*

HENRY MILLER

* Henry Miller, *The Wisdom of the Heart*, pp. 95–96. Copyright 1941 by New Directions Publishing Corporation. Reprinted by permission of New Directions Publishing Corporation.

Introduction

I believe fear is the single emotion we need to understand most. It is one of the strongest forces we will ever feel inside ourselves, and one of the strongest motivations in individuals, groups, and societies.

Fear can unnerve, cause ulcers, kill us; it can destroy marriages and organizations and it profoundly influences our national and international politics. Advertising campaigns are built around it and people live their lives caged in by it. We cannot ignore it, but we try desperately to do just that.

In writing a book about fear, I am in pursuit of the fear in myself and I am searching for a broader exploration of the fears we all experience. I want to know as much as I can about my own fears so I can use them for my own growth. At the same time, I want to provide others with as many tools as possible—tools for facing and dealing with the fears they experience.

This book is drawn not so much from a deep well of fears in my own life as it is from an intense involvement with the study of personal growth—my own and others—and how fear and growth are related.

In the past five years of my life I have been involved in what is popularly called the human potential movement and I have convened classes and groups in interpersonal communication, creativity, problem solving, creative writing, sexuality, and personal growth.

Last year, with the help of my colleagues at *Center for Studies of the Person*, I wrote a book called *How Do You Feel? A Guide to Your Emotions.* In that book, forty of us talked about thirty-one different emotions, from acceptance to trust, in a very personal way. The book was an exploration of feelings in our society, how we experience them, how they make us behave, and what some of us have learned about them.

It was during the research and writing of that book that it became clearer than ever how low a regard we have for our emotions and how little attention we pay to them. It is a tragedy of our educational system and a deep loss to each of us personally that we do not learn more about our feelings as we are growing up. As we mature it becomes harder and harder for some of us to acknowledge and express our emotions, especially "negative" ones like fear, anger, or sadness. Such a rich and powerful part of our lives lies deep inside, covered by years of ignorance and neglect, our own as well as others. Our emotions are neither "good" nor "bad;" they are ours and we can experience them and talk about them without being afraid or ashamed of them *and* without acting on them, if we choose.

All of this became very important to me during my membership at the Center and while writing *How Do You Feel?* After I had finished that book and could look more objectively at it, it was clear to me what the most important, most pervasive, emotion was. My feeling then underlined and confirmed the experience I had had in the groups and classes with which I had been involved over the years. I can remember that after the first couple of years of leading various kinds of learning experiences, a similar feeling would be aroused in me when it was time to end. Usually, I had been involved closely with these people for weeks or for several intense days and, on leaving, I wanted to give them something. Always it was courage.

I remember saying to one group that I wished I could give them a five-pound box of courage from which they could draw strength whenever they needed it. I had seen, time and time again, and continue to see, how fear ripples through us when we are on the verge of something or someone we want. I have seen and felt the "shells" people build around themselves, afraid to venture out to meet others, much less turn inward to look at themselves. Often I have grown sad and cried on experiencing people missing one another, passing by as if they were in darkness, neither with the courage to smile nor touch or even look, though they deeply wanted the contact.

In each case, to grow into something we want for ourselves or to make contact with another, we need to risk—to move through a barrier of fear. We are afraid of looking stupid, being weak, of what others will think, of making mistakes, of being hurt, of being rejected, of change, the unknown, of surrender, and afraid of each other.

I know I can't give anyone else courage; it wouldn't be courage if someone else gave it to you. But I can wish it for others, and I do. Because we are afraid, all of us, day in and day out. From birth to death, fear travels with us. It excites us, holds us back, traps us and, in a curious way, waits inside us to challenge us and lead us on to bigger parts of ourselves. It keeps us from what we want, but it shows us what we want the most. It can paralyze us or it can spur us onward. Fear and its brother, rage, being two of our most basic, most animal-like emotions, affect our bodies like no other emotions can. Ultimately, fear can kill us, through ulcers or heart attack. Or perhaps, even worse, we can live a stifled, caged-in life, suffocated by our own fear of venturing out to know and love others.

The question of how we as individuals can move through our fears to personal growth and to intimacy with others is, I believe, the single most important question we can ask ourselves. How to move through the fear between groups of men and women and nations to a posture of trust and community may be the most important question that confronts the human race.

This book, then, is one small flashlight pointed in that

direction. It represents one man's hope that by learning about the fear we all experience, we can use that knowledge to overcome our fear and enrich our lives. Together we will confront the things some of us are afraid of; we will turn the spotlight full on fear to see what it is, how it affects us, and how it differs from—and is linked with—other emotions. Finally, we will explore a wide range of different perspectives on fear, different ways to look at and deal with that great shadow that touches us all.

Unmistakably this is a book about fear. But turn it inside out and it is a book about growth and loving.

PART ONE

Definitions of Fear

CHAPTER 1

We all are afraid

No man, woman, or child goes through many breathing hours on this earth without experiencing fear. Love may escape us, hope may have deserted us, we may avoid sadness, and put away our anger, but fear lurks in all the corners of our lives.

It comes to us in different ways—a nightmare, tall buildings, a shadowy figure, a drop in the stock market, an angry parent, a prediction of the future, a lover leaving. Each of us deals with it differently—withdrawal, nervous laughter, screams, anger, apathy, a gradual retreat from the things we want. And, within, we confront different fears in different ways.

It is possible that our first experience in the world is fraught with fear; that we are pushed from the womb, from a world that is soft, warm, quiet, and comforting, into a nightmare of bright lights, harsh sounds, cold air, and physical pain. A new human being is born, but we are tense with fear, our face contorted with pain and confusion, our eyes closed. Perhaps our first emotion outside the womb is fear, our first response to hide.

We are taught to fear: "Fear of the Lord is the beginning of wisdom." We are urged to cast out fear: "All we have to fear is fear itself." Fear has been utilized by dictators, politicians, academicians, psychologists, writers, movie makers, as well as salesmen, and advertising men to bring about results they desired.

We all have fear in common—to be human is to be afraid. It is a thread that runs through our lives. Often the way in which a person deals with his fear becomes the measure of his life. It may be on the battlefield, the football field, in a marriage, in front of a canvas, or in a business office. If we are lucky, we are aware of our fears and when those moments of choice come, those moments of reaching out or withdrawing, we can choose based on our own instincts of what is best for us. The first step is to get introduced, or re-introduced to our fear. In his book *Conquest of Fear*, Basil King wrote about the fear that wound its way through his life:

> When I say that during most of my conscious life I have been a prey to fears, I take it for granted that I am expressing the case of the majority of people. I cannot remember the time when a dread of one kind or another was not in the air. In childhood, it was the fear of going to bed, of that mysterious time when regular life was still going on downstairs, while I was buried alive under sheets and blankets. Later it was the fear of school, the first contact of the tender little soul with life's crudeness. Later still there was the experience which all of us know of waking in the morning with a feeling of dismay at what we have to do getting up; the obvious duties in which we have perhaps gone stale; the things we have neglected; those in which we have made mistakes; those to which we have willfully done wrong; those which weary or bore or annoy or discourage us. Sometimes there are more serious things still: bereavements, or frightfully adverse conditions, or hardships we never expected, brought on us by someone else.
>
> It is unnecessary to catalogue these situations, since we all at times in our lives have to face them daily. Fear dogs one of us in one way and another in another, but everyone in some way.
>
> I am ready to guess that all the miseries wrought by sin and

sickness put together would not equal those we bring on ourselves by the means which we perhaps do least to counteract. We are not sick all the time; we are not sinning all the time; but all the time all of us—or practically all of us—are afraid of someone or something.

It strikes me as strange, on looking back, that so little attempt was made to combat fear by religion. In fact, as far as I know, little attempt was made to combat fear in any way. One's attention was not called to it otherwise than as a wholly inevitable state. You were born subject to fear as you were born subject to death, and that was an end of it.[1]

What is it that we are afraid of? What are some of the things that nag at us in the middle of the night? What are some of the catastrophic expectations we have for ourselves and our loved ones? What is the mortar and brick of the walls we build around us?

There is a great temptation to just answer: "everything." It is sad but probably true that, collectively, there isn't anything we aren't afraid of.

Benjamin Rush, a physician, seemed to have had the situation under control as he wrote in a publication called *Medical Inquiries and Observations upon the Diseases of the Mind*, published in 1927.

He wrote: "There are [sic] so much danger and evil in our world, that the passion of fear was implanted in our minds for the wise and benevolent purpose of defending us from them. The objects of fear are of two kinds. 1. Reasonable. These are death and surgical operations. 2. Unreasonable. These are thunder, darkness, ghosts, speaking in public, sailing, riding, certain animals, particularly cats, rats, insects, and the like."

There has been a lot more serious and thorough research into our fear, however, and into the things we're afraid of, particularly as children. I think it's worth examining the few fears we are "born subject to," how they grow and change as we become older children and young adults and, finally, the sophistication and complexity they gain in our adult lives.

We are born fearing only loud noises, sudden, unexpected

---

[1] Basil King, *Conquest of Fear* (Hollywood, Calif.: Newcastle Publishing Co., Inc., 1972), p. 1.

movements, and falling. Some of what we learn to fear after that is necessary for our physical and emotional survival in our culture—some is not. Keep in mind that, besides those categories of innate fear, the things you and I are afraid of today we have learned; presumably then we can unlearn them.[2]

In an often referred to study of sources of fear in children, Stanley Hall found that 1,100 boys and girls were afraid most of thunder and lightning. Approximately one third of the children tested gave thunder and lightning as a specific response.[3]

Other responses, in order, were persons, reptiles, darkness, death, domestic animals, rats and mice, insects, ghosts, wind, the end of the world, and water. Further down on the list and mentioned by only a small percentile of the children were such fears as self-consciousness, solitude, shyness, and ridicule, the latter two being mentioned by only one percent of those questioned.

In a later study, responses of 50 boys and girls were broken down in categories and charted by age groups, three to six years old, seven to eight, nine to ten, and eleven to twelve. The highest percentile answer was 27.3 of those tested—three- to six-year-olds afraid of animals. In the eleven- to twelve-year-old group, those answers had dropped to 11 percent. The younger children showed a relatively lesser fear of bodily injury and physical danger; that fear tripled by the time the students were eleven.[4]

Older children also seemed to fear uncanny or strange circumstances more: the dark, being left alone, lights and shadows. Fear of scoldings and reprimands that left a sense of guilt or failure showed a sharp increase as children got older. A relatively low percentage of children questioned were afraid of illness or death of people close to them or of startling events and loud noises, though these did increase with age.

The researchers noted that there were no outstanding differences in response between boys and girls. Nor were the differences significant when related to IQ.

These two studies were made in 1897 and 1933 respectively.

[2] Paul Thomas Young, *Emotion in Man and Animal* (New York: John Wiley & Sons, Inc., 1943), p. 168.
[3] Ibid., p. 387.
[4] Ibid., p. 388.

Two studies reported in 1968 and 1970 show a marked difference in responses.[5]

Responses of children in elementary school still showed bugs, animals, ghosts, the dark, and thunder and lightning high on the list of danger signals. But personal relations and politics also had become something to worry about. War, the Communists, being ridiculed or ostracized by others—more sophisticated, more social fears were being reported by children.

Carole Klein's study reported in the *New York Times* (see note 5) claimed that children were afraid of more things and different things than most parents were aware of: for example, dying, 81 percent; someone close dying, 80 percent; animals, 75 percent; house burning down, 73 percent; people following, 73 percent; and being kidnapped, 70 percent.

It seems safe to say that the fears of our children—and our own, as we will see—are becoming more "civilized," more urban and more interpersonal.

Our fears and those of our children are related to different needs and take place in different settings than those of our grandparents. There is a new self-consciousness among many young people and some adults; there is more attention being paid to self-actualization, which is at the top of Abraham Maslow's hierarchy of needs.

In more primitive cultures and in the most basic parts of ourselves, we are concerned with and fearful of things connected with primary needs such as survival, food, and shelter. When those needs are met we become concerned with social acceptance. Self-actualization is a "luxury need" in a way; it can be dealt with only when all the other needs we have are met. In striving to realize all that we are there is a feeling of reaching for a new part of the self, indeed a new kind of person. With those new extensions of self, there are new kinds of fear.

John Vascancellos, a bright young assemblyman from California, talked about this consciousness as it relates to fear and education in a May, 1973, speech:

> I suppose the old educational experience is that which comes down on the youth, so as to give them the painful sense that

---

[5] Carole Klein, "Who's Afraid of the Big, Bad World," *New York Times Magazine*, September 22, 1968; *Science Digest*, December, 1970.

they have to deny their feelings, lock away their questions, and stay quiet for fear of looking stupid. When I think of kids asking questions, I think of myself going through school and being afraid to ask for fear of showing I didn't know the answer, for fear of having the wrath of the power structure come down on me. I was always the brightest kid who got all the awards, but I didn't ask questions because I was afraid to. New consciousness education for me really means education that affirms the right of a child not to be afraid of himself or herself, not be afraid to declare his own needs and wants, recognize the body, the mind, and the emotions as a whole composite of what it means to be human, no one of which is less basic or less human than the other.

In different settings and under different conditions, fears change. More and more we pack ourselves into cities. Eighty percent of us live in an urban environment; many of us do not know our neighbor. This congestion, this great gathering of people to live together, offers the opportunity for more person-to-person contact and satisfaction, but it also is a breeding ground for fear.

In February of 1974, the *Watchtower*, a religious publication, published its version of what was happening in American cities and how people were responding.

> More and more the United States is becoming a terror-ridden "armed camp."
>
> Fear pervades "all levels of U.S. society," according to a Gallup poll taken in 1973. One person in three in the big cities and one in five in the suburbs has been mugged or robbed, or has been the victim of burglars or has had his property vandalized in the past year. Four persons in ten are afraid to walk alone at night even in their own neighborhood.
>
> Some people believe that the way to cope with violence is to be ready to use violence in return. As a result, in Detroit, the nation's top crime city, it has been estimated that there are 500,000 handguns, one for every third man, woman and child. The situation is not much different elsewhere. People live in fear.[6]

In the same month, *Time* magazine was passing along this bad news: According to an FBI report, more than half the crimes

---

[6] *The Watchtower*, Watchtower Bible and Tract Society of Pennsylvania, February 15, 1974, p. 1.

of burglary, auto theft, and larceny of over $50.00 are not reported. Despite that contention, the rate of reported crimes continued to rise. Forcible rape, for instance, increased from 18.6 per 100,000 women in 1960 to 43.5 in 1972. The number of people who reported they were afraid to walk alone at night increased from 34 percent in 1965 to 42 percent in 1972.

The *Watchtower*, predictably, said that Satan himself was the villain in this scenario. Few of us would buy that answer, right? More than you think.

The Center for Policy Research, an agency that studies social trends, released a study made in 1973 which claimed that 48 percent of the American people were convinced that the devil existed, a rise of 11 percentage points in nine years. An additional 20 percent of the people questioned considered his (or her) existence probable.

One of the researchers involved in the study attributed the increased belief in the devil to a "mood of uncertainty and stress, when things seem to be falling apart and resources seem limited for coping with it."

The same survey found that people's certainty in the existence of God was down 8 percent. While the devil's stock was going up, God's dropped from 77 to 69 percent. While the existence of Satan or God, in one form or the other, is not clear, it is clear that we're afraid of both.

The fear of God is instilled in some of us at an early age. The Psalms tell us:

> The fear of the Lord is the beginning of wisdom. (111:10)
> The friendship of the Lord is for those who fear him, and he makes known to them his covenant. (25:14)
> Serve the Lord with fear, with trembling kiss his feet, lest he be angry, and you perish in the way; for his wrath is quickly kindled. (2:11)

Millions of people grow up with the fear that if they step out of carefully prescribed limits, they will be judged and experience one kind of hell or another. Fear, guilt, and guarded behavior are a good possibility when one places too much reliance on the value systems and intent of any authority figure—God, your father, or your boss.

When we live in fear of what someone else will say about us or do to us when we act on our own instincts, it is impossible to develop a sense of responsibility, maturity, and/or self-worth.

David Cole Gordon, in his book *Overcoming the Fear of Death*, relates joy, religion, and fear:

> It is difficult, if not impossible, to live spontaneously and positively with joy if we are constantly fearful of losing all we have and are haunted with a sense of futility about all existence. Nor are these dark feelings attenuated by any of the religious teaching; they are rather enhanced by them, for the Christian religion, in particular, is premised upon the view that it is the life hereafter that really counts: this earthly life is important only insofar as it is a gateway.[7]

So the great judgment day awaits. Whether this concept has any real meaning for you or not, it is hard to escape the judgments we go through in day-to-day life: our parents judge us, our spouses judge us, our bosses evaluate us, our teachers grade us, critics criticize us, our colleagues judge us—all the while exerting the pressure to conform and be rewarded. The fear is of being different, of being yourself, of being something other than what the authority figure wants, and of being alienated because of it.

We are afraid of authority, sometimes with good reason. Political leaders, for instance, have a unique position of being able to inspire love—or fear—in people who have never met them. These two reports from *The Los Angeles Times* give some hint of the power and fear potential in being a political leader:

> His [Agnew's] attack on the press and TV brought ecstatic praise from Tricia Nixon: "The Vice President is incredible. I feel I should write him a letter. He's amazing, what he has done to the media—helping it [sic] to reform itself . . . I think they've taken a second look. You can't underestimate the power of fear." [8]
>
> Madame Tussaud's Waxworks—one of London's major tourist attractions—passes out questionnaires to its visitors. Last year's selections for the exhibit or wax effigy that created the most

---

[7] David Cole Gordon, *Overcoming the Fear of Death* (New York: Macmillan Company, 1970). Copyright © 1969 by David Cole Gordon; reprinted by permission of Harold Matson, Co., Inc.

[8] *Los Angeles Times*, October 2, 1973, Sec. 1, p. 2.

"hate and fear" apparently were a strong indication of the men who hold, or have held, power in the world. In first place was President Nixon, followed by Adolf Hitler and Jack the Ripper, while tying for fourth were Defense Minister Moshe Dayan and Libya's Moamar Khadafy.[9]

The consciousness that we are in a more interrelated and interdependent world than ever before leads us to feel a great deal of dependence on and vulnerability to world political leaders. The knowledge that one nation can destroy another in a matter of minutes and we as individuals do not have much affect on that decision is indeed fear-provoking.

Whether we believe in the devil, God, or political leaders, or none of the above, the things we fear change as we grow older. We leave bugs, thunder, and dogs behind (most of us) and graduate to being afraid of making a fool of ourselves in public, being rejected in love, making mistakes, failing, dying, losing esteem, and a long, long list of other, more complicated, things.

The fears we lose, or rather, learn about, seem to be concerned with nature and our own bodies. When we mature and grow, and learn more about our place in the world and what goes on in the world around us, and gain some degree of self-control, we can leave those fears behind. Then, we believe, we have to pay attention to succeeding in relationships with the opposite sex, making some mark in our chosen field, maintaining friendships and professional relationships, achieving financial security, and holding our own self in a high regard.

You might say that our fears move out from a body-centered, sensual, natural world into a social, interactive sphere of other individuals and groups and ultimately to a space where our fears become more centered in our view of ourself and our relationship with those closest to us.

For example, a 1974 survey reported that Americans are more afraid of speaking in public than they are of insects, heights, or illness. Forty percent of 2,500 people questioned said they would be afraid to speak in public; women were more afraid of this than men. People who earned less or were less educated were even more concerned about speaking in public.

[9] *Los Angeles Times*, January 18, 1974, Sec. 1, p. 2.

Your station in life and how you relate to the rest of society has a great deal to do with what your fears are. Children are dependent on adults, in varying degrees, for emotional support, food, housing, clothing, approval, and/or legal sanctions. This dependency makes them vulnerable, in their eyes, to the world at large and thus they are more capable of fear. The more control they take over their own lives, and the more authority of their own they exert, the less fearful of others they become.

Racial minorities are in an unfortunate position, too, relative to social fears. Deemed inferior, systematically held back in education, employment, housing, and medical care, and subject to a different kind of law enforcement than most white Americans, blacks, browns, and other minorities are subject to different kinds of fear and different intensities than whites will ever know.

James Baldwin, in this excerpt from *The Fire Next Time*, writes about the intense fear some blacks experience and the effects it has on his race:

> [The Negro past] of rope, fire, torture, castration, infanticide, rape; death and humiliation; fear by day and night, fear as deep as the marrow of the bone; doubt that he was worthy of life, since everyone around him denied it; sorrow for his women, for his kinfolk, for his children, who needed his protection, and whom he could not protect; rage, hatred and murder, hatred for white men so deep that it often turned against him and his own, and made all love, all trust, all joy impossible.[10]

The excerpt from Baldwin's book says, in a few words, how fear can permeate a man and can lead to disillusionment and hatred. Can we love when life is so filled with fear? Can we trust anything or anyone when our life experiences have taught us little else but fear?

While children and other subjugated people have a particular susceptibility to fear, they have by no means any license on it. Fear reaches everyone, including those who are "successful" in the public eye—entertainers, artists, and politicians.

In a newspaper article last year (1974) several Hollywood stars said what they were most afraid of.

---

[10] Excerpt from *The Fire Next Time* by James Baldwin. Copyright © 1962, 1963 by James Baldwin. Used with the permission of James Baldwin and The Dial Press.

Lloyd Bridges is most afraid of dying. "I've no doubt that the fear of death is man's most basic fear—the one he discovers first and the one that's most difficult to overcome," Bridges said.

Clint Walker said he was afraid of making the same mistake twice and not learning from it. Anne Francis was afraid for her children; that something might happen to them or her and she wouldn't be around to take care of them.

"Fear of getting a pot belly scares me to death," Lyle Waggoner, of the Carol Burnett Show, said. "That's what keeps me doing exercises, jogging, and watching the calories."

Mitzi Gaynor is afraid of heights. June Haver is afraid of being crippled or incapacitated in a way that would keep her from doing or experiencing things.

Ed Asner, the tough news director on the Mary Tyler Moore Show, answered: "Lacking courage when it's needed. Not having the courage to speak out or act decisively would truly bother me."

Acting decisively bothers film director Richard Lester, too; he said in a recent interview:

> In 1963–64, I made three films in one year, luckily without the chance to think about it and worry. Ten years later one starts to be more cautious. And the more films you make the more you realize how many films you can't do. Perhaps that's the prerogative of youth—leaping into an area you don't know, feeling sure you can conquer it. They say that when you get older you're supposed to get more intelligent but it's not true, all you get is just more frightened, and it's very difficult to make any film in an atmosphere of torture.[11]

Perhaps caution does come with age and with it also comes, for some, senility. Golda Meir, the former prime minister of Israel, expressed what many people reaching into their sixth or seventh decade must be thinking about:

> I'll tell you at once my only fear is of living too long. You know, old age is neither a sin nor a joy: there are lots of unpleasant things to old age. Not to be able to run upstairs, not to be able to jump. . . . Yet, one easily gets used to some things. Mere physical handicaps are not degrading. What is

[11] *Los Angeles Times*, Calendar sec., September 23, 1973.

degrading is losing one's lucidity, becoming senile. Senility . . . I've known people who died too soon, and it was painful. I've known people who died too late, and it was equally painful. Listen: I feel insulted when I see the collapse of a fine brain. I don't want to undergo that insult. I want to die clearheaded. Yes, my only fear is living too long.[12]

Howard Baker, the Senator from Tennessee, touched on a fear that affects most of us when he commented on his feelings about the operations of the Central Intelligence Agency:

> I do not think there is a man in the legislative part of the government who really knows what is going on in the intelligence community, and I am terribly upset about it. I am afraid of this lack of knowledge. For the first time, I suppose, in my senatorial career, I am frightened. I am generally frightened of the unknown.[13]

Others, unknown to the world, the "average" people who live next door, harbor the same kinds of fears as the famous. Our fear shows up in scores of different ways—we are afraid of what will happen if we integrate our schools so we stone young black children; we are afraid of losing our children or a spouse so we smother them with protective, controlling "love"; we are afraid of saying what we really think or feel about things so we sit silently at public meetings, muttering under our breath about how bad things are.

Behind so many public events that make the news and private happenings between two people in their own home is the question: What are you afraid of?

I asked a group in San Diego to answer that question, a white, middle-class PTA that had invited me for a talk in June of 1974. Here are some of their answers:

"I'm afraid people aren't really listening to what I'm saying."

"I fear loneliness in old age."

"I must be afraid of being physically attacked in the dark because I'm not relaxed in a quiet, dark area."

"I'm afraid of a dog named Max."

---

[12] Oriana Fallaci, "Golda Meir: On Being a Woman," *Ms.* Magazine (April 1973), Vol. 1, No. 10.

[13] *Washington Post*, October 7, 1974, p. 3.

"I'm afraid to be wrong—therefore, I'm hesitant to confront a teacher or person who can influence my children and be offended by what I say."

"I fear I won't be accepted by others; I fear I don't really accept myself."

"I'm afraid of how people will respond to me. I'm afraid of how society tries to draw out introverts."

"I'm afraid of missing experiencing all parts of myself, losing myself to someone important to me, to a crowd, to pressure from people I care for."

"Rejection."

"I am afraid of heights."

"I am afraid of being without human contact."

"I fear (1) parenthood—how we might or might not influence our children, (2) failure, (3) being accepted."

"I fear being at the edge of something high."

"I'm afraid of being in an elevator alone. I'm afraid of too-busy people."

"I'm afraid of being turned upside down."

"I fear failing those who trust me, through my own fault."

"I am afraid of poor health in old age."

"I am afraid of snakes and heights."

"I'm afraid of being alone at home at night—all night."

"I fear I have no fears that I know of."

"I am afraid of people shouting and swearing, snakes, cats."

"My greatest fear is speaking in front of a group of people because I cannot think quickly on my feet and often can't communicate exactly what I feel."

"I'm afraid of being alone . . . of death."

Loneliness . . . harm . . . being wrong . . . being rejected . . . responsibility . . . heights . . . old age . . . not being myself . . . being alienated . . . death—the list goes on and weaves through the history of a person's experiences, if we—or they—could ever know them all. And our fears tell us something about the way we see the world through those two small windows that are uniquely ours.

On quite a different occasion, during a weekend group on

sexuality, I broached the area of sexual fears with the participants. Here are some of their answers to the question, What are you afraid of?:

"I am afraid people think I'm a stone."

"I am afraid of being alone, being rejected, failing, and hurting."

"I am afraid people will think I have homosexual tendencies; not that I act that way, but look like a person who may be homosexual."

"I am afraid to learn about my sexuality."

"I am afraid to surrender."

"Sometimes I am afraid of not meeting a woman's expectations. It is fairly easy for me to think I am responsible for keeping my partner happy."

"I fear: impotence, marriage, possessiveness (hers and mine), loss of respect, loss of privacy."

"I'm afraid of loss of erection when long foreplay (not reciprocal) is required to make a woman ready for intercourse."

"I'm afraid to talk to sexual partners about my sexual needs during intercourse or how we can improve the sexual relationship."

"I fear my capacity to have orgasms may disappear."

"I'm afraid of the pain that comes with the growth in becoming more of a person."

"I'm afraid to have someone become dependent on me."

"I'm afraid of being judged and pigeon-holed by people I care about because of sexuality."

"I'm afraid of being me, absolutely."

"I fear: aloneness and isolation, disapproval, lack of love, criticism, closeness, loss of control over my emotions, mistakes, risk-taking, being spontaneous, never finding love and sexual fulfillment."

"I am afraid of being ridiculed about my sexual desires and impulses."

"I am afraid of being rejected as inadequate without a chance to change or defend myself."

"I'm afraid my penis is too small."

"I'm afraid of not 'performing' for my partner."

"I fear, and am drawn to, touching other men, loving them, caring for them, and being accepted by them."

"I am afraid of not being attractive to men."

"I am afraid of focusing so much of my energy on sex that I lose myself as far as other interests and people are concerned."

"I am afraid of having intercourse so casually that it becomes meaningless."

"I am afraid of my attraction to other men and women; wanting to express it, claim it, make room for it, enjoy it, and be proud of it without destroying the one most vital relationship of my life."

"I am afraid of not getting all I want and need sexually. I am afraid of not being as intimate in the other parts of the relationship as I am in the sexual part of it."

"I have a fear of getting old, fat, and undesirable."

"I am afraid of losing women as friends (potentially) because they think I am *only* sexual."

"I am afraid of letting go . . . and it keeps me from coming."

The area of sexual fears is worthy of special attention, not only because it is an area that this culture covers up and perverts so thoroughly, but because in many ways the sexual act is analogous to life itself. Some of the things we can learn about the joy of sex are lessons that hold true for life.

We'll deal with this later in the book; perhaps it is sufficient to say here that fear is the greatest barrier I know of to complete sexual fulfillment—fear of failure, fear of growing old and unsexy, fear of being not enough, fear of not satisfying your partner, fear that you'll seem foolish or strange.

Sex reflects, sometimes in great magnification, our preoccupation with success, achievement, and ego and our emphasis on youth.

Fulfilling sex is wrapped up in intimacy. Intimacy means at least a partial surrender, a surrender of power, authority, secrecy. It is a true, deep sharing of one being with another; it takes time and it takes risks.

The courage to become involved is needed to overcome two basic kinds of fears. In our society one is more often experienced by men, the other by women. The fear of living alone, of ultimately being isolated from anyone to love, most often felt by women in America, leads many times to throwing one's self into a relationship so thoroughly that the self-concept is sacrificed to the will of the other person or to holding the relationship together.

Males most often experience another kind of fear, one that could be seen as almost the opposite. It is a basic fear of death, but in relationships it takes the form of a fear of being absorbed, swallowed, possessed, and in being absorbed, losing identity.

Many American men shy away from intimacy in a relationship because of lessons they learned from a possessive, over-solicitous mother. The smothering of a child with too much "love" can lead to a strong fear of being swallowed up in a permanent embrace.

We have a curious push-pull attitude about intimacy, as we do with many of our fears. We want it badly and at the same time we are afraid of it.

One friend wrote me about his fears of love and loving:

> I often see myself running in all directions, away from those things I'm afraid of. Or is it to something I want and can't ask for? I don't like being there—in that scrambling around, fragmented state—and I seem to strike out at people whom I think put me there. I try to get even and use all my weapons to hurt them, even my most effective—withdrawal. And when I am alone, without anchor or support, without being able to touch or be touched, my biggest fear swells up inside—that I can't love. Because I don't. And that's the fear that means most everything to me now.
>
> I stop when I say that because it is hard for me to face. It is easier to reach out in small ways and love a little and then say, "See, I do love," but underneath that kind of social reaching out is the spectre of, "Do I really love anyone? Will I ever love anyone?"

This man is not alone in his fear of not being able to love. The fear of entering into a relationship and allowing yourself to reveal yourself and share yourself is one that troubles most people I know. It is accompanied by so many understandings, so many steps out and back, so much hard work at communicating—always shadowed by the fear that something we offer will be turned down.

awkward, afraid,
i set out to meet you

> *my first attempts are slow and hard*
> *a word*
> *a finger*
> *a smile*
> *a hand*
> *a feeling shared*
> *an arm*
> *i am not hurt yet*
> *and you are so soft*

That was the way meeting one woman felt to me, in the very first stages. There is the feeling of offering a little bit and if it's not rejected, offering a little more.

My friend Ralph Keyes, in his book, *We, the Lonely People*, wrote about his and others' fear in this way:

> We sit alone, or hidden in a crowd, and wonder how it was that we got so cut off. With luck, we have someone else to blame it on—Dr. Spock, perhaps, or Richard Nixon. Perhaps a program takes our mind away: if only we had a revolution; if only better people got elected; if only all would return to God and flag. Then I wouldn't be so lonely.
>
> But it doesn't work. Because it's we who cut ourselves off, by the things we value which make it unnecessary to bump into each other: the cars, the computers, the suburban castles.
>
> But these are just tools, reflections only of something more basic cutting us off from each other, which is fear. Fear. Pure and simple. Fear of intimacy. Fear of rejection. Fear of getting too involved. Fear of ourselves, fear of what they might find if we let others peer too deeply inside.[14]

Inherent in the nature of intimacy, as I mentioned, is a surrender of sorts. Surrender, in its largest sense, is death.

In talking with people and in researching this book, I have gotten a thousand different answers to the question, "What are you afraid of?", but I guess if any of us talked to another person long enough and got past some of the superficial fears, most of us are afraid of that ultimate surrender. Death is the bottom line for most of us. A belief in life after death or life in another form after this one is a part of some lives and is some solace I'm sure. Even

---

[14] Ralph Keyes, *We, the Lonely People* (New York: Harper & Row Publishers, 1973), p. 140.

so, there is the fear that what one believes will not come to pass.

David Cole Gordon calls the fear of death "the mother of all fears" and believes that much of our American culture is, at heart, a response to our fear of dying.

> The culture which is then derived has, in turn, a causal effect which nurtures the fear of death. . . . Everything man does, builds or creates is in large measure designed to assuage his conscious or unconscious fear of oblivion, and the anguish of the realization that his life and death may be meaningless. So he attempts to succeed, make money, build monuments, do good work, have children, and prolong his physical existence as long as possible.[15]

The ultimate surrender—giving all I have to an all-encompassing unknown. And losing it; losing control, losing consciousness, losing will. And becoming, what? Vapor? Dust? Or in a space where the concept of becoming means nothing?

That surrender is something I hope to talk about again and again. In a curious way, in the paradox of paradoxes, to surrender—wholly, even passionately—is what we want and what we are most afraid of.

We are afraid to die. We are afraid to love. We are afraid of life itself. We are afraid to fail and afraid we will succeed. We are afraid to get too close and afraid we will stay too far away. We are afraid to fully commit ourselves to something or someone and afraid that we won't.

We are afraid of each other and afraid of ourselves; yet, we desperately want one another just as we want our own unique self.

How can we resolve these paradoxes? How can we move toward satisfaction? intimacy? joy?

I have come to believe in fear as a key to growth. The things I am afraid of provide me with directions, just like the points of a compass. That is a way I want to move. This is something I want to do, because I'm afraid of it.

I want to know my fears; more, I want to embrace them, to enter into a relationship with them.

---

[15] Gordon, *Overcoming the Fear of Death*.

CHAPTER 2

Fear is . . .

"Fear is a knot in my stomach and a pounding heart."
"Fear is not saying what I really want to say."
"Fear, for me, is my husband, in a drunken rage."
"Fear is a movement at night in my bedroom."
"Fear has mostly to do with failing at something I want to do badly."
"Fear is a dream I have in which I'm being chased by a crowd of angry women with meat cleavers."

We define our fears in many ways. We can think of fear as a sensory experience, an avoidance, a person or other animal, an event—real or imagined—or a thought or fantasy.

Though it can take many forms and mean a myriad of different things even to the same person, fear is perhaps the most powerful of our emotions. It has shown itself to be stronger than hunger, thirst, or sex, at least temporarily, and over the long run, can interfere with the fulfillment of each of those basic drives.

It is, at the same time, primitive and complex. We share fear with other animals though we alternately wrap it up with anger, guilt, frustration, dependency, and inferiority and compound it with anxiety and phobias.

I'd like to examine some of the basic facts about fear—the bodily changes that take place in response to fear, some of the games we play when we're afraid, the behavioral responses men and animals make to fear. Hopefully this will be a primer of basic animal fears, from which we can see what we as humans have added and see if there are lessons to be learned about our more sophisticated fears.

Basically, men and animals experience fear in the face of present, anticipated, or imagined danger or pain. There is a real or imagined threat to one's well-being or survival and our basic, most primitive response is to flee and conceal ourselves.

Our bodies get ready for this flight immediately. Our heart beats faster, increasing our blood pressure; there is a general tension of the entire muscular system; eyes become dilated to make things clearer and nostrils flare to admit more odors; more sugar pours into the bloodstream for energy and more adrenalin is secreted; there is even a tendency to rid the body of excrement, to lighten the load it will carry. There is a massive and rapid preparation for flight or, if necessary, defense. It is interesting that researchers find little difference between bodily responses for fear and for anger.

One of the important physiological differences relates to blood sugar and strength. In fear, adrenalin pumps into our system and causes a contraction of the blood vessels. Sugar is released from our liver and our muscles, actually making the muscles weaker after an initial burst of energy. This accounts for the feelings of malaise, weakness, or even exhaustion after a fearful experience and helps us understand how chronically fearful or anxious people often suffer from lack of energy. In anger, our body produces noradrenalin, which causes sugar to be released from the liver but not the muscles. The use of the blood sugar by the muscles is not retarded, giving us more strength in anger than in fear.[1]

Normally, when the object causing fear is removed or dealt with in a way to reduce fear, these bodily changes subside and functions return to normal. If, however, the individual continues in a fearful or anxious state and the body continues to respond, it is as if he were continually running his motor. The body begins to strain under the pressure. Eventually headaches, hypertension, high blood pressure, or ulcers can result, as well as other diseases linked to emotional distress.

This happens when fear remains with you, despite the fact that what made you afraid is no longer around. You are, in a sense, carrying your fear—once present, but now in the past—into your future. There is an important element of time—past, present, and future—that runs through all of this, and how we relate to time has a great deal to do with our fear. In the section on anxiety, we'll explore that in more detail.

This powerful emotion, then, born of experiences and injuries not only in our immediate past but in the course of our evolution, "has developed into a portentous foreshadowing of possible injury and has become, therefore, capable of arousing in the body all the offensive and defensive activities that favor the survival of the organism." [2]

Responses to "real" threats are necessary for survival. As pedestrians, we need to see the car speeding toward us as a threat to our safety. If we want to ride, somehow we need to know that the wild, unbroken mustang in the corral is a threat to our safety.

To respond with fear and avoidance in cases like those is not only natural but necessary. But it is possible that a response to an experience can become generalized into an attitude, a "mind set," into which a person fits all similar future experiences as fearful. After one negative experience a person may favor a negative response to certain objects, people, or situations. We may come to fear all cars or horses or we may fit black men or dominating women into our slot labeled "danger." Both animals

---

[1] Albert Deutsch, ed., *The Encyclopedia of Mental Health* (New York: Franklin Watts, Inc., 1963), p. 549.

[2] Walter B. Cannon, *Bodily Changes in Pain, Hunger, Fear and Rage* (New York: Harper & Row, Publishers, 1929, 1963). Reprinted by permission of Bradford Cannon.

and men do this generalizing and it is one of our worst enemies, particularly in interpersonal relationships.

All this has to do with learning, of course. With fear, the old saying "What you don't know won't hurt you" is far from the truth. More to the point is "A little bit of knowledge is a dangerous thing." We experience that one kind of person will hurt us and we apply that to others we see as being that way, based on little or no knowledge of the situation in the present. We have learned to be afraid.

Situations that combine the familiar with the unfamiliar are more likely to make us afraid than something that is completely unknown. When you know just enough about something to perceive or suspect some potential danger, but not enough to know what is really going on or be able to control it, you are likely to become afraid.

If, for instance, an infant sees a dark, funnel-shaped cloud approaching, he may be curious, even attracted to its shape and movement. An adult, on the other hand, would run to shelter. The infant lacks any background knowledge about tornados, is not aware of the danger, and does not experience fear.[3]

The same could be true in personal relationships. A young and relatively innocent young woman could fall in love and become wrapped up in a relationship with an older man, who might send out definite danger signals to a woman with some experience. The older woman, in this example, knows enough to be afraid. Whether this is her gain or her loss is another question.

We do gain more fears as we get older; that is, we lose some and gain others and if we don't leave the fears of childhood and young adulthood behind, it is possible to become a prisoner of fear in our own bodies.

Fear can act as a big stop sign in our development and, though some traumatic experience, can cement itself down in the middle of our lives, telling us that we can go no further, that we cannot continue to grow. Perhaps you know people who act like they have never left their adolescence or their teens; fear can be an important part of that stopping and staying in the same place.

One of the important tasks in therapy is to re-visit those

---

[3] Paul Thomas Young, *Emotion in Man and Animal* (New York: John Wiley & Sons, Inc., 1943), p. 386.

stop signs and gradually, by trusting and gaining more individual power, move on.

This process is sometimes complicated and confusing because our fears are complicated and confusing. It is not always clear what our fears are, where they came from, or how we got them. Fear can spring directly from a harmful experience; it can be associated with a person, animal, or object; we can transfer fears from one unpleasant thing or person to another; we are evidently biologically predisposed to fear certain types of things more than others and our level of fear has something to do with our belief that we can somehow cope with the situation. Several experiments and reports by psychologists, psychiatrists, and other students of human behavior help explain these points.

Psychologist John B. Watson, some fifty years ago, conducted one of the studies most often referred to in this area when he set out to condition an 11-month-old boy to fear a white rat.[4]

Watson chose a normal, healthy boy—Albert, the son of a Baltimore nurse—for this experiment. He first presented him with a rat, rabbit, monkey, dog, and masks, all of which the boy took some pleasure in.

On subsequent presentations of the white rat, Watson clanged two steel bars together, startling the infant and causing him to rear back, catch his breath, and begin crying. After two such experiences of reaching out for the rat and being startled by the loud noise, the boy fell forward on his face and whimpered. A week later, Albert would not touch the rat.

After seven similar trials, Albert had transferred the innate fear of the loud noise to the rat and the presentation of the rat *by itself* caused him to cry, turn, and crawl away quickly.

Albert was tested again, five days later, and Watson found he was now also afraid of other white, hairy things—a Santa Claus mask, a fur coat, and the rabbit.

In a very short time and to an intense level, Albert had done something we all do: he had *learned* to associate what before had been neutral or even pleasurable signals with an event that alarmed him and he began to generalize. What earlier brought him pleasure, now—without real reason—made him afraid.

[4] Ibid., p. 168.

Watson maintained, as do many behaviorists after him, that if we somehow knew the minute-by-minute history of a person we could determine where his or her fears came from and know better how to deal with them. Others believe that an elaborate history is not necessary, that fears can be dealt with in the present and that behavior can be changed by working directly with the behavior itself and ignoring the causes. Later in the course of the book we will look at some of this behavioral work.

Other experiments have shown that our fears do not spring solely from our interactions with our environment, but that we are "ready" to fear some things more than others.

An English psychologist, C. W. Valentine, conducted an experiment with his own daughter, an experiment similar to Watson's, in which he tried to teach his daughter to fear two unfamiliar objects—a caterpillar and a pair of opera glasses.[5]

Valentine found that his daughter was much more afraid of the caterpillar, after its accompaniment with a loud whistle, than she was of the opera glasses with the same noise. He concluded that there was something different and special about the caterpillar—its texture, its hairy appearance, its movement—something that set it apart as a danger signal. He said that the attitude toward the caterpillar, and other similar animals, was an "unstable" one and we humans are much more ready to respond fearfully to certain kinds of signals than we are to others.

Other work has supported his thesis. In an article in the *New York Times Magazine*, Maggie Scarf explores this possibility in interviews with contemporary psychologists. She asks:

> Are we as species . . . genetically "prepared" to learn to fear certain classes of stimuli? Are we neurally "prewired" for acquiring fears about certain objects or situations, which have perhaps affected human survival over the long course of evolutionary history?[6]

The article answers yes, based on some research and writings by Dr. Martin Seligman, a psychologist. Seligman co-edited a book, with Joanne Hager, called *The Biological Boundaries of Learning*. In an essay at the close of the book

---

[5] Maggie Scarf, "The Anatomy of Fear," *New York Times Magazine*, June 16, 1974, p. 16.

[6] Ibid., p. 17.

Seligman points out that individual human beings are biologically ready to fear some danger signals more than others because of thousands of years of evolutionary learnings.

The same is true for other animals. Birds, for instance, not only learn to turn wheels for food in a scientist's laboratory—as their ancestors never did—but they also learn to migrate away from the North Star when the weather turns cold—something their ancestors have done for generations. "All of this learning may not be the same," Seligman concludes. We can more easily relate to his examples for humans.

You or I may have learned to be afraid of an aerosol can exploding in our face if we burn it or puncture it; this is something our great-grandfathers never had to face. Yet both your great-grandfather and you may be afraid of the dark, something we are much more ready to do as a species. Our original adaptation was for food gathering during the daylight and at night getting together with others in a shelter and sleeping, while predatory animals roamed about in the dark. This, Seligman points out, makes it easy to believe that you and I are "conditioned" to be more afraid of the dark—and animals, lonely exposed places, and perhaps even strangers—than we are of auto accidents or stumbling on the rug and breaking an arm.

Modern kinds of fears that we may be plagued with in crowded cities and in the midst of sophisticated machinery have no evolutionary basis. Therefore, the authors say, they are less likely to trouble us, less likely to be the source of our deepest phobias and more easily "unlearned."

On the other hand, our fears of animals, of strangers, particularly of a different skin color or build, of being exposed and alone, of being closed in and captured—all these may have a more primitive base. They may be tied to evolutionary learnings that are much more deeply engrained and more likely the source of tension and deep fears.

"We respond, with disproportionate force, to those objects and events which have, during the long course of our evolutionary past, been reliable predictors of danger," Ms. Scarf concludes.[7]

This leads to some interesting contradictions. In the first

[7] Ibid., p. 20.

part of this book we read that, with an ever-increasing crime rate, "fear pervades all levels of the U.S. society." That four out of ten people are afraid to walk alone in the streets at night. That we are afraid of being robbed, mugged, raped, or killed by a stranger.

What kind of reality are those fears based on?

The FBI reports that 18,520 people were murdered in 1972; most of those killings, as any student of homicides knows, come at the hands of a spouse or other family member or during a lover's quarrel or as a result of a romantic triangle. In short, someone you know very well is much more likely to kill you than is a stranger.

In the same year, the National Safety Council reported that 17,000 people died in accidental falls. We are killing ourselves by falling off ladders and out of buildings at nearly the same rate we're being murdered!

In the same year, 56,590 Americans were killed in automobile accidents—more than three times the total killed in violent crimes.

The FBI estimates that 100,000 people were injured that year in a mugging or robbery, a tragic figure, to be sure. But, according to the National Center for Health Statistics, 24 million people were injured in accidents in the home; 4 million of those injuries resulting in serious disabilities.[8]

Though the figures have gone up recently, there is really a very small chance that any one of us will be the victim of a violent crime, particularly violence perpetrated by a stranger. The chances are much greater that we will be hurt or killed in our own car, by falling off the ladder while painting the roof, by slipping in the shower, or while repairing the electrical wiring at home.

We are paralyzed by fear of each other, yet we cause much more harm to ourselves. Perhaps our fear of each other is out of line with reality, but there may be some important reasons why.

One factor is predictability; we tend to fear situations (and perhaps people) who are unpredictable. We do not know what is going to happen, so we are afraid of it, whatever it is. If only we

---

[8] Ibid., p. 10.

could control it. Control, too, the feeling of some degree of mastery over a situation, or a person, tends to reduce our fear. The more helpless and dependent we are, the more susceptible we are to fear. Two recent experiments point this out.

Psychologist Seligman, using rats and electrical shock, found that unpredictable pain induced more stress and fear than did the same amount of pain that was predictable. He explains his experiment:

> Consider two situations in which hungry rats are pressing bars to obtain "rewarding" food pellets. In the first condition, we present a tone that is paired with electrical shock. When the tone is on, as he rapidly learns, he is going to get that jolt. And so he'll feel fear at the signal and he'll stop bar pressing.
>
> On the other hand, he'll have learned, also, that when the tone is off, he is perfectly safe. This will put him in a quite different position from, say, another rat who is receiving exactly the same number of tones and shocks but who is getting them randomly. There is for the latter animal, no relationship at all between tone and shock. For him, the experience is one of complete unpredictability. There's no stimulus which tells him he is all right (as the absence of the tone does for the first rat) and not going to get shocked. There is, in other words, no sanctuary.[9]

Among the eight rats who could not predict their pain, there were six with stomach ulcers; they spent a good deal of time huddled together in a corner of their cage, apparently in a state of unrelieved fear. The other test group appeared more normal in behavior and developed no ulcers.

As Seligman points out, the fact that we cannot predict our pain tends to stretch out time and makes our fear more pervasive. It is not possible to relax and stop worrying.

Violence at the hands of a stranger has this sort of unpredictability. You cannot say if or when the person following you will harm you or if there is a mugger waiting in the doorway ahead, hence you are on guard, tensed, ready for defense or flight.

Accidents, in the home, on the other hand, have some degree of predictability. We will not fall off a ladder unless we

---

[9] Ibid., p. 20.

deliberately climb it; we won't slip in the shower without getting in and getting wet, and we won't run our car into the tree unless we get in and start the car. It is that sense of not knowing what another person is going to do to us that makes us more afraid.

Perhaps that is why some people try to control situations and other people, so they can reasonably predict what will happen. Experiments also have shown that when we have some degree of influence over a given situation, we are more likely to cope with it than if we are not. The belief that we can influence a situation, or at least cope with it, not only lowers our stress but allows us to endure an unpleasant experience where others, without that belief, would not.

A Yale psychologist, Jay Weiss, experimented with two groups of rats in 1968. He found that a group that had learned what he called a "coping response" to the administration of an electrical shock (turning a wheel or jumping on a platform) developed far fewer stress ulcers than a group who could do nothing. Both groups of rats received the same shock.

Another study, this one with humans, showed that merely the belief that one could influence the situation one was in, lowered the emotional response and made the experience less threatening. (Separate studies, with university students in Poland, have shown that fear lowers the pain threshold significantly, causing a person who is afraid to "hurt more" than one who is not.)

Belief plays a large part in our story of fear. There are fears, as we have seen, that we are born with and some fears we are more receptive to than others. But the large majority of fears we experience and the fears that do the most to keep us from becoming our full selves are invented. They are man-made and man-perpetuated. The kind of fear I'm talking about is a belief, a fantasy, a thought. It is rarely in the present, nearly always in the future. Even when the past tugs at us, telling us of painful experiences, it is the fear that they will happen again in the future that drains away our power. This is uniquely human; it is fascinating and tragic that we have invented and continue to invent the building blocks of one of our most powerful motivations.

In some deep animal part of ourselves, our basic fear is

there—that our survival is threatened, that our body will be maimed—and our bodily responses wait to be triggered, as they did millions of years ago, when we were threatened by a wild animal or a warrior from another tribe or group. But how often does modern, urban man face that fear? Besides war and situations we deliberately put ourselves in, how often do any of us come face to face, in the present, with a situation that threatens our existence? Rarely, especially when we compare those times to the fears we invent, and project into our own future.

We subject ourselves to the fear of failure, the fear of rejection, the fear of being punished, the fear of looking foolish, the fear of loneliness, and the fear of death. If we can think of these fears as our own creations and learnings that we have had, we immediately find them smaller and easier to deal with.

CHAPTER 3

Anxiety and phobias

On the perimeters of our fear, on the edges of what psychologists like to call "authentic fear," are phobias and anxiety.

If we think about the development of our fears as a path that we travel, from low intensity to high, our anxiety would be at the beginning. It might be a meadow with the grass just a little too high to be comfortable and dense enough so that we worry about stepping on a piece of glass, if we were barefooted, or maybe even coming across a snake. There might be several areas where the grass is beaten down, indicating several starts at a path, but it is not clear which one we will take. So we wander around a bit, somewhat aimlessly, looking for the right way to go and worried that we won't find it. Also there can be the feeling of excitement that we are doing something new and refreshing and we cannot anticipate what this holds for us. Our body responds to this with a certain amount of tension and, in a minor way, with some of the same responses it would if we were afraid of something specific.

Eventually, we do start down one of the beginning paths. Our fears might be characterized as things along the way that bring out stronger reaction than our anxieties, things that cause us to stop for a while and think about turning back. We might see a dark form moving alongside the road or hear something following us. We might see an animal peering out at us from the woods just ahead. Or, we might be afraid of what we think will be waiting, whatever it is, beyond the sharp turn in our path that is coming up.

If an animal does spring out to claw at us or bite us or if a tree limb crashes to the ground around us as we turn the corner, we are shocked and scared to the point of screaming and turning and running to some sanctuary. Shaken and tending to whatever physical and psychic wounds we have, we are too afraid to go on. Any pair of eyes peering at us suspiciously is enough to stop us in our tracks. Turns in the road where we can't see what lies beyond become so threatening we will take them very cautiously if at all. Perhaps we will let someone else go first. We have developed phobias.

This fantasized account of the relationship of anxiety, fears, and phobias may help give you a feel for what each of these is and how they develop; however, they deserve a closer, more definitive look.

Anxiety is fairly new; at least recognizing and talking about it as a separate entity is new. From the Latin, *anxietas*, it commonly connotes an experience of uncertainty, agitation, and dread. The original Latin usage also implied a suggestion of strangulation; it is probably no coincidence that anxiety is evidenced in many people by a general constriction of the neck muscles, a condition that can become chronic. One doctor, in fact, described the case of a stock broker who became excessively anxious and developed, among other bodily symptoms of fear, a pulsating enlargement of the thyroid gland. Eventually, it turned into a goiter.[1]

---

[1] Paul Thomas Young, *Emotion in Man and Animal* (New York: John Wiley & Sons, Inc., 1943), p. 390.

Though anxiety may be nothing new to stock brokers, it was not talked about generally in psychology books until the 1930s. Freud first introduced the term to therapists in 1894, when he described anxiety neurosis as a separate syndrome. Early on, he believed anxiety was the outcome of repressed sexual tensions; that we held down our sexual desires, cut them off from any kind of normal expression and turned them into a general plague of anxiety.

Freud later broadened his version of what anxiety was, and included factors in our outside environment as causes, but it remained for latter-day psychologists and writers to fully define it for modern man. After all, it does seem to be the curse of modern man; in the 20th century we have isolated this little piece of man's fears and carefully nurtured it into something of our own.

There are a wide range of fears, in terms of their intensity, from a mere nagging apprehensiveness to a screaming, uncontrollable terror. While anxiety is on the low end of that scale, it still has the real potential to disrupt the flow of everyday life, cause a poor performance in school, work, or sex, affect health to the point of illness and eventually cause death and, generally, to keep one from moving through life in a comfortable, "efficient" way.

Anxiety is more general, vague, and overall than a specific fear. It has a tugging, nagging quality about it that is sometimes subtle, sometimes more direct. Some psychologists call it "a foreboding of evil." Others think of it in more positive ways.

Paul Thomas Young describes it in this way:

> . . . it is a more persistent state, a chronic foreboding of evil or harm. The anxious individual is tensely set for pain or injury, illness, death, disgrace, or humiliation to be visited upon himself or some other person. He usually recognizes fairly definitely the source of the impending misfortune over which he worries. This is not always true, however, for anxiety sometimes takes the form of a chronic apprehensiveness about no specific thing. Sometimes, instead of there being no definite anxiety object, the individual in this state worries over a whole succession of different things, some of which actually offer real grounds for worry.[2]

[2] Ibid., p. 61.

Psychologist Harry Stack Sullivan wrote that anxiety is "always the fear of disapproval."

There is not always agreement on whether anxiety is inherently a good or a bad thing; it may be what you make of it.

Fritz Perls, in *Gestalt Therapy Verbatim*, calls anxiety

> the excitement, the *élan vital* which we carry with us, and which becomes stagnated if we are unsure about the role we have to play. If we don't know if we will get applause or tomatoes, we hesitate, so the heart begins to race and all the excitement can't flow into activity, and we have stage fright. So the formula of anxiety is very simple: anxiety is the gap between the *now* and the *then*. If you are in the now you can't be anxious, because the excitement flows immediately into ongoing spontaneous activity. If you are in the now, you are creative, you are inventive. If you have your senses ready, if you have your eyes and ears open, like every small child, you find a solution.[3]

In their book, *The Risk of Loving*, Joseph Simons and Jeanne Reidy seem to second Perls' definition:

> Although it is unreasonable to suggest that major fears overshadow all our normal activities, it does seem true that during most of our day we are preoccupied with the future. It may be fear of a friend's gentle rebuff. It may be fear that someone will discover we are not really comfortable in his company. It may be fear that we have not done well on an examination. It is as if we are designed to move to the future rather than stay with the present. The future too easily becomes the present in a way which creates worry and tension.[4]

Psychologist and author Rollo May also acknowledges the duality of anxiety:

> Anxiety occurs at the point where some emerging potentiality of possibility faces the individual, some possibility of fulfilling his existence; but this very possibility involves the destroying of present security, which thereupon gives rise to the tendency to deny the new potentiality. . . . If there were not some possibility

---

[3] Fritz Perls, *Gestalt Therapy Verbatim* (Moab, Utah: Real People Press, 1969), pp. 2–3.

[4] Joseph Simons and Jeanne Reidy, *The Risk of Loving* (New York: Herder and Herder, 1968), p. 20.

opening up, some potentiality crying to be "born," we could not experience anxiety.

What these statements about anxiety have in common is the concept of expectation. Perls' definition appeals to me the most; his analogy of anxiety with a stage performance is easy to identify with. I don't have to go any farther than my own experience to see how the concepts of performing and stage fright and insecurity in my roles apply. When I am thinking about a performance, but don't know how it's going to be received—in fact expecting that I will get tomatoes—I experience a kind of anxiety that often insures my performance will be awkward, hesitant, or veiled. In this way, my own anxiety helps set up what I was anxious about—it is a self-fulfilling prophecy.

When I can let go of my concentration on the future, on the response, then my act is much more likely to be free, flowing, and truer to what I want to say or do. By not worrying about success or failure, whatever those terms mean, I am helping to assure my success. The concept is, in Zen terms, by letting go of what I want, I get what I want.

Whatever your own concept of anxiety is, it is just that, your own. Anxiety (as well as fears and phobias) is related to your own unique experiences and personal characteristics. Whether it comes from internal conflicts or from relationships with the others around you or your environment, anxiety reflects the kind of personality you have developed through your infancy and childhood.

Many people I have talked to about their anxiety say that a fragmentation or lack of focus seems to be either the cause or a result of anxiety. It's a little like being in the meadow in the analogy used at the beginning of this chapter; there are many paths to choose from and some aborted beginnings. The fragmentation and inability to choose only leaves one in the meadow.

One man called it "a nameless fear that creeps into me" and noted that it often had positive side effects for him:

> In a way anxiety is a good thing; it's not always bad. In fact, I don't have many anxiety experiences when I don't recognize them as a kind of creative energy. My organism is telling me that I ought to be focusing on something, giving more attention to

something than I am. If I'm watching TV and I've got something else that I'm anxious about, it creeps up on me and keeps making me think "I shouldn't be here" and of course at some point I've got to break, I've got to stop doing the distracting thing and focus.

A woman I interviewed talked about the same fragmentation:

> I'm first aware of my anxiety when I try to read a book and my mind wanders. But I don't want my mind to wander so I try to get involved in other tasks, but I can't. My mind won't stay with it. My energy and vitality are being directed inward and I don't like it. The harder I try to direct my energy outward, the more fragmented and frustrated I become. I seem to be unable to control what I want to do. I am frightened. This anxiety to me is a huge, undefined fear. I don't know what I'm afraid of so I don't know how to face it. I have a tremendous feeling of holding in, but I don't know what it is I'm holding in.

A little anxiety is not a problem. It is normal to be anxious; there is no one I know who does not experience one degree of anxiety or another almost every day. When it does become a problem is when it seeps into most of your waking hours, when it begins to control your life instead of you being aware of it and using it for your own good. It is possible that a vague but powerful anxiety can begin to take over your body, mind, and emotions, that it can develop into a problem of sizeable proportions. When you are concerned about what is going to happen to you or what people think of you most of the time, and when there is little connection between the things you're worried about and what is really happening, then anxiety is a problem and it is time to seek help.

We might say that anxiety becomes problematic or harmful to us when it goes unchallenged. We cannot help but know anxiety because there are times in our lives when, like it or not, we are going to have to do something new. To succumb to the anxiety then, to not deal with what it is pointing out to us, is to let it gain some measure of control. To acknowledge the anxiety we have and to deal with it in one way or another is the beginning of some learning experience for us.

Robert Nixon gives an excellent description of this process in a child in his book *The Art of Growing:*

There is no question but that fear itself is a variety of unhappiness, and further, a variety that everyone avoids as much as possible. There is also no question but that some new experiences are fear-inspiring. The eighteen-month-old toddler who falls into the deep end of a swimming pool for the first time will be scared for some time after he has been fished out, and with good reason. But the same toddler placing a box on a chair, then climbing up and standing atop the rickety tower for his first view of the top of the mantel, will not be scared. He will feel some degree of anxiety simply because he has tried something new, and it will be so minimal that only a rather skilled observer will be able to identify it—unless, that is, his mother suddenly comes in from the kitchen, sees him on his precarious perch, and emits a frightened maternal shriek. If she is that scared, he too will be scared; and if enough of his early exploratory attempts meet the same kind of parental reaction, it will not be long before his anxiety is consistently tinged with fear, whether or not the object of his exploration is inherently fearsome. In other words, it seems entirely probable that at first the child—any child—is a fearless explorer, except when his explorations bring him into contact with something that is genuinely fear-inspiring; but as time passes he is too often taught to equate all explorations with fear. If he learns this lesson thoroughly, he will react with tension-tinged fear to almost any new experience; his parents will probably think his fears are evidence of unhappiness, and they will do what they can to make him happy once again. If they, in their turn, are successful, they will soon have a child who is afraid of new experiences, afraid to explore, afraid (worst of all) of his own anxiety, the feeling that lets him know he is confronting something new.

At the other extreme is the individual who has not learned to equate anxiety with fear. When he encounters something new (assuming it is not inherently dangerous or threatening) he too reacts with the physical changes associated with the body's preparation for action: increased heart rate, rapid and shallow breathing, tightening of muscles, perspiration, often a trembling of the hands. But if these changes are not accompanied by a feeling of fear, we are more likely to say that the person is feeling excitement of heightened interest or active curiosity than to say that he is experiencing anxiety. In other words, it seems very probable that the element of *emotional discomfort* that we usually consider an inherent part of anxiety is, for the most part, learned.

(After all, most of the new experiences we discover are not only not inherently dangerous—they are downright inviting.) Obviously this is not true of the anxiety one feels when facing a genuinely threatening situation, and probably it is not true, either, of prolonged anxiety, whether its source is threatening or not. But it does appear to be true of most of the day-by-day anxiety we experience in the process of growth.

To summarize, then, anxiety is the normal emotional response to anything new or unexplored; it need be accompanied by a feeling of fear only when the new is in some way inherently dangerous, because of parental and/or societal teaching it is much too frequently accompanied by fear whether the new is dangerous or not, and since it seems to constitute unhappiness it is also guilt-provoking. When it occurs without fear or guilt it is indistinguishable from excitement or heightened interest and it leads directly to exploration of, or experimentation with, the new; and when it is needlessly tinged with fear and guilt it tends to prevent exploration or experimentation. In other words, *anxiety uncontaminated with needless fear leads to growth*, while *anxiety associated with irrational fear prevents growth*. Most American young people have been taught to associate anxiety with fear and to control their anxiety with guilt. As long as such a control is operative, growth toward maturity is difficult indeed.[5]

The unknown seems to be the villain—the unknown outside of ourselves and the unknown parts of ourselves we don't know and perhaps don't want to know. Whether our unknowns, our undiscovered villains are real to others or not, they lurk there, waiting to be challenged, or maybe befriended.

Knowing, for sure, is incompatible with anxiety. We could propose knowing as some kind of cure-all then. To know is to rid ourselves of anxiety. To know about everything out there ahead of us is to rid ourselves of fear.

But there is always something new—a first day at school, making love for the first time, meeting a new man, playing a game for the first time, tasting a new wine, giving birth to your first child. If we knew all we could predict. If we could predict and know it would come true, we would no longer be surprised or excited.

[5] From *The Art of Growing*, by Robert E. Nixon, pp. 130–32. Copyright © 1962 by Random House, Inc. Reprinted by permission of the publisher.

We cannot know life, we can only move toward it. We cannot be fully prepared. We can only try to know alienated and unconscious parts of ourselves, to gather in the unknown within us to make ourselves more whole for the journey we all make.

Whether or not anxiety helps or hinders that journey is debatable. Studies of anxiety as well as individual experiences contain many contradictions. Some analysts maintain that anxiety is uniquely human, that animals are afraid and man is anxious. This springs from our ability of self-transcendence, our definition of time, our filtering of danger signals through our interpretation of meaning of past, present, and future. In animals there is fear and reaction. In man there is fear, pause for meaning, and choice.

Anxiety is called "the mother of our drive to know" and "one of the engines of our creativity," that "exhilarating and frightening discontent that strengthens our urge to go on and yet sees the dangers of the enterprise."

On the other hand, it restricts our ability to let go and enjoy ourselves. It is the sticky binding agent between our animal and civilized self that will not let us surrender to our completely natural self. Unbridled, we are a threat to our own civilized picture of ourselves, so we stew in the conflict.

It could be the very *angst* we need for art, for positive expression, but in some it is just as strong an urge for destruction, of self and others. Perhaps we are driven to know by our anxiety, but generally we learn more easily when our anxiety level is reduced.

Perhaps it is enough to say that a little anxiety goes a long way, particularly when we think of it as Freud did, as a longing, a constant reminder of our helplessness without love and protection.

Along this path of fear we are traveling, phobias are the stop signs. They are the "do not enter—wrong way" warnings we see on the freeway ramps. They are the signals, based on some reality in the past and, in most cases, long since useless, that tell us not to proceed.

The difference between a "normal" fear and a phobia is not always distinct and depends upon the culture, the person, the context, and the environment. It would be unusual for a man from Wyoming, for instance, to develop a phobic reaction to elevators or subways; we might expect this from a New Yorker.

Most of us, somewhere along the way, have been afraid of the dark, being left alone, becoming seriously ill, or certain animals. In most cases our reactions to these fears have not been too intense nor have they lasted for a long time.

These are several yardsticks we might hold up in trying to determine whether we can call a person's response a phobia: (1) there is a prolonged preoccupation with the object or situation feared; (2) the reaction is inappropriate, that is, not based on any reality; (3) the reaction to the danger signal is very intense.

An example: all of us would be frightened to some degree if someone pointed a knife toward us in a threatening manner. To be afraid in that circumstance is an appropriate, normal response.

To respond in a fearful way, with extreme physical reactions of fear, to a knife lying on the table, to a store window display of knives, or to a realistic picture of a knife in a magazine would be called phobic.

A person plagued by a phobia or phobias may have extreme physical reactions. The reactions are what most of us would experience when we are afraid but taken a step or two farther. The phobic person may experience heart palpitations, difficulty in breathing, rapid breathing or choking sensations, nausea, vomiting or diarrhea, shaking, shuddering, sweating, dizziness, insomnia, and/or increased sensitivity to sounds and lights. An object or situation not even noticed by one person may touch off reactions in a phobic person as if his or her life were at stake.

Phobic reactions are more common in children than adults; in fact most children develop at least a temporary phobic reaction sometime in their childhood. As we unlearn these danger signals and know more about the world, our extreme fears of certain objects and situations are left behind.

While some phobias can be a direct result of an experience with a person, animal, or situation, many psychiatrists believe that the stimulus that sets off the phobic reaction is only a symbol and a false target for that person's fears.

This becomes a difficult thing to generalize about, because each person's fears are his own and spring from his unique personality and experience. There are fairly common phobias, however, as well as some general dynamics we can apply to most of them.

In his book, *How to Overcome Your Fear of Flying*, psychiatrist Marvin L. Aronson points out some of the common danger signals or stimuli that may cause phobic reactions: Animals, sharp instruments, travel, confined spaces, heights, crowds, going crazy, darkness, lightning, thunderstorms, fire, falling asleep, death, being left alone, stage fright, touching, blushing, heart attack, blood, hospitals, fights, weather, shadows, cancer, syphilis, germs, cats, school, and fear (phobophobia).[6]

Aronson goes on to list what he calls the "psychodynamics of phobias," which I would like to summarize here. It was important for me as I read Aronson's chapter, as a way of learning as much as I could about myself, to try to identify with as much of it as I could. In fact, I "tried on" a lot of different fears during the writing of this book. I realized that phobic reactions are different in degree and that by exaggerating my own fears and my own reactions and taking on what I have learned about phobias, I could learn a lot about my "normal" fears. In short, perhaps we can learn more about ourselves by not pushing phobias away to a safe distance, to learn from them under a microscope as it were, but by taking as much as we can into ourselves and owning it, if only temporarily.

One basic feature of phobias, as far as Aronson is concerned, is that a conflict between a person's impulses and his "irrational conscience" already exists within the phobic person. The irrational conscience develops in early childhood and is the result of childhood misperceptions and exaggerations of parents' "shoulds," "can'ts," and "mustn'ts." As we become adults a more mature conscience and judgments of our own take over for the most part, but this childhood judge of our actions never leaves us completely.

This judge, which is used to bossing us around and finds us now with different impulses than he would like, may begin to feel very aggressive, even hateful toward other parts of us. This

---

[6] Marvin Aronson, *How to Overcome Your Fear of Flying* (New York: Hawthorn Books, Inc., 1971).

aggression could be directed against our whole self, against specific acts or fantasies, or against parts of our body, as is common in sexual phobias. This part of ourselves that is the judge varies, of course, in strength and durability from person to person. It may clamp down on just one or two of the things we do or it may have a whole host of ways to make us feel guilty.

All of this conflict rages on unnoticed most of the time. Pleasurable fantasies we might have or even pleasant sensations associated with a forbidden impulse are repressed. As long as we keep our new, free self down, we won't have to be punished by that judge, our irrational conscience.

The phobic reaction is started, much like a match lighting a powder keg, by a seemingly innocuous situation or object. The stimulus revitalizes our already existing conflict and kindles our already existing anxieties. While we may be aware of our anxiety in the situation, we are not aware of the relationship between the situation and the struggle going on inside us. To admit this would mean we would have to deal with our conflict.

So, to avoid coming to grips, we attach our fears to something external—horses, knives, flying, driving cars. This is called displacement; we take a conflict inside that we are afraid to face and name an outside villain for it.

Instead of realizing that our fear springs from within, we focus on external threats and maintain to the world that someone or something is all too ready to bring us harm. It is much easier to deal with an external threat we can identify and point to than it is to cope with our own self.

Sometimes we may even regress to an earlier form of behavior—an extreme dependency on a spouse or other person close to us—to adjust and avoid the responsibility of making our own decisions.

Escape is the answer for most phobic persons; upon removal of the external threat, the anxiety symptoms go down *and* the underlying conflict remains repressed. One good reason for this behavior is that we can use the danger signal as a kind of "off" and "on" button for our anxious reactions and we do not have to remain in a constant state of anxiety and conflict.

Aronson points out that counselors have to do "a great deal of detective work" to find out what fears lie at the base of our phobic behavior. His opinion is that most of the conflict can be traced to three sources: fear of retribution for sexual desires and fantasies, fear of retribution for aggressive thoughts, or fear of being left alone in the world.[7]

We can think of anxiety and phobias in the same package. In our definitions of anxiety we saw two common threads: the vague prediction of harm and the tension of conflict within the self. We might say that anxiety appears when something we are about to do or experience calls forth a sort of warning signal within ourself. It might be a warning based on our sense of reality—that what we are about to do will, in fact, hurt us. Or it may be a warning based on our conscience, carrying with it old threats of punishment.

At this critical warning signal, we have several alternatives: we can act in spite of our anxiety and take the risk of going against "shoulds" that are someone else's or based on different realities; we can retreat from the anxiety-producing conditions by withdrawing; we can stay right at the warning point and experience the tension and unrest that accompanies it.

Though few of us consciously choose to stay anxious, millions of us choose not to deal with the conflict—the same choice, in a way. Fear and tension begin to take their toll on the body, sapping us of strength, spontaneity, and naturalness. When we refuse to acknowledge that tug of war within us, we are not only denying ourselves a new part of ourselves, but we are robbing ourselves of vitality and energy as well. If we choose not to deal with anxiety, it will deal with us; it will control us because we ignore it. If we choose to deal with our anxiety by retreating, it is possible that our "choice" will lead to a phobia of one kind or another. Unable to stand the tension and constant conflict that intense anxiety brings with it, we may withdraw and focus instead on one or two symbols (or situations) as fear objects. We will retreat from the general discomfort of anxiousness into a relative safety and focus our fear on an object or experience that, from then on, carries with it a phobic reaction. That's why it often takes so much investigation for analysts to determine the original roots of our fear; we have withdrawn from the difficult

[7] Ibid.

conflicts within and focused our fear on something or someone outside.

When we act out of our fears (and in a succeeding chapter we will look at our responses to fear), those actions can be directed at ourself, our father, mother, brother, our husband or wife, a nationality, or a whole race of people. Whatever person or group of people we keep at a safe distance, that we reject, avoid, or defend ourselves against, fear is the likely reason. We may be afraid of ourselves, of what we would do if we followed our real impulses—a sexual advance or a hot-tempered verbal attack—or we may be afraid of the harm or ridicule that person or group might bring down on us.

You might try this out on yourself. Think of a person or a group of people (a racial minority, for instance) with whom you avoid contact or real involvement. Admit that you are afraid of something. Try and determine what it is—ridicule, physical harm, rejection, etc. Then think about and discuss, if you can, how acting out of your fear is making you behave. What are you depriving yourself of? What are you gaining? How would you like to change?

Again, this is not to say that a certain amount of anxiety and/or fear is not normal and, in some circumstances, healthy. But when we act out of our fear blindly, without the consciousness that we have a choice and without our best interests at heart, we are experiencing less of life than we could.

CHAPTER 4

Fear and other emotions

Wrapped up in our package of fear, sometimes as co-sponsors and sometimes as fallout, are other emotions that feed our fears or go along with them. Exploring what they are and how they are related helps us define fear even more. In this section I would like to look at the relationship of fear to anger, guilt, dependency, insecurity, and frustration.

Anger and fear are two of the most powerful forces that drive men and other animals. Our physical reactions to those two emotions, as we have noted, are remarkably similar. You may have noticed a dog when it's angry—hair up, teeth bared, eyes wide, body tensed, and all of its attention intently focused on the object of its anger. Its reactions to fear are remarkably similar and most of the time, without knowing the cause, it's hard to know whether an animal is afraid or angry.

Both fear and anger are preparations for action and are

reactions to a threat of one kind or another. Either emotion arises from a situation that is likely going to cause flight or conflict, both extreme situations that will require a lot of energy and effort on our part. In that way it makes sense that our bodily responses are nearly the same.

We have probably seen fear turn to anger, in ourselves or someone else. It is easy to imagine a fearful animal being pursued and cornered and the fear quickly turning to rage, in an all-out effort to defend its life. Often the difference in reactions—whether to be afraid or angry—may be only one small element in the situation, and the same situation might evoke fear in one person and anger in another.

While it is easy to imagine how close these two are linked in a threatened animal, such as our own dog, it's more difficult to see their relationship in interpersonal relations. Take, for instance, a party at which a couple is approached by a third party, a man. This person starts to express his interest, in indirect but definite ways, in the woman. Her escort is threatened. Most of us can probably identify with this situation and, if we can imagine ourselves as the escort, can see that we could be afraid or we could be mad, or both. We could get mad because we're afraid. We could retreat (flight and concealment). We could leave the situation alone or try to take the woman with us. We could get angry at the other guy and at the same time be afraid to express that anger, or we might get angry at the woman. Later, when we're home and the whole situation doesn't seem as threatening as it did, we can get mad at ourselves for feeling so threatened (afraid).

While anger and fear are closely related in their causes and their effects, most often they are counterparts between two people. Anger is, in its expression, a display of power—its counterpart is fear. We can see this in many relationships between men and women. In our society, as well as in most of the rest of the world, men are vested with the trappings of power and the actual power; they have the roles and the symbols of power in institutions and families. They have the titles, the money, the recognition of others, and generally exert the most influence in decision making.

We might say the same things about relationships between

parents and children, white and minority races, teachers and students, bosses and employees, and officers and enlisted men—in each there is an imbalance of power and the potential to inflict punishment.

As we will explore further in the next chapter, the fear of punishment is one of our most powerful determinants of action. There are times when we will do most anything to avoid what we consider or imagine to be a painful punishment. We can see that it is nearly inherent in each of those relationships mentioned that authority or power establishes fear. Whenever one half of the relationship holds more power than the other, there is the fear that, in one way or another (punishment, withholding of affection, withdrawal of support), that power will be used.

Of course this varies a great deal in individual relationships and institutions, but power is power and it is naive to think that power plays are not going on most of the time in most relationships. Each of us is the subject of some kind of power and the purveyor of power as well.

This has heavy implications for all of us. I don't believe any of us think we operate at our best, most creative self when we are afraid, yet the fear of punishment is one of the conditions we unconsciously accept and operate under for most of our lives.

All of this might be expressed in the sentence "I have power over you so you must fear me." But I find fear and power a curious coupling and it might be expressed in many cases in this way: "I fear you so I must have power over you." When a person or a group has an investment in authority over another, it may spring from the fear of what the subjugated person or group would do if the power (control) was removed. "I am so afraid of you—leaving me, hurting me, being smarter than me, taking my mate—that I must keep you under my thumb."

We can see this in politics, relations between the races, marriages, the classroom, and countless other situations. While the person under the influence of another's power is afraid of punishment, the person with power fears the loss of control.

Fear and anger can mingle solely within an individual as well as between persons and groups. For instance, some part of myself may be angry at another person for not showing up on time for an appointment. But another part, a larger part, is afraid to express that anger, afraid of what I will do or say when and if I really let go; afraid of what the other person will do in return or think of me when I get mad. For many of us, especially women, anger is hard to express. We grew up with the notion that getting mad was against the rules and, at some level, we are afraid that if we get mad we will be punished.

Judith Wells, in an essay titled *Daddy's Girl*, wrote about her own coupling of fear and anger:

> Nothing is more startling to a Daddy's girl than to find herself in revolt against her Daddies. Because of her intimacy with the desire for approval from her Daddies, she finds it painful to make a clean break with them.
>
> Underneath, I based most of my personality on masculine approval. Any criticism from a male brought me a haunting sense of guilt.
>
> This Little Girl infects many females because she is nurtured by so much of society as by ourselves. She has no age limit. . . .
>
> As a Little Girl, I found that I had based my personality for such a long time on approval from authority figures that they were my personality. I experienced "psychic" smallness because I had never defined who I was or what I wanted in life; my only sense of identity stemmed from Daddy's approval.
>
> The real tragedy of the Little Girl, then, is her inability to define herself in her own terms, select her own goals, and feel her life has significance without Daddy's support.
>
> It would be great if the Little Girl could join the Women's Movement and instantly become a self-sufficient woman. I have found that my Little Girl personality is not shed so easily, and that my rebellion against my Daddies has its own peculiar Little Girl cyclic rhythm: compliancy towards a man—simmering hate—explosion of outrage—anxiety over having stepped over the line—fear of reprisal—compliancy towards a man and the cycle begins again. Because the Little Girl has suffocated her own desires so completely in favor of her Daddies, her potential for rage is volcanic once she questions the belief that "Father knows best." Yet for myself and probably for most Little Girls, each explosion is followed less by a sense of triumph than by anxiety and fear of reprisal. . . .

Perhaps the most important part to remember about all this

is simply how closely anger and fear are related and that each can come out of a threatening situation. Though it is not always true, when we get mad we can usually look under the surface and find out something we are afraid of; if it is not the prime motivation, it will at least help us understand our anger.

Frustration can lead to fear; we can see that in things we do every day. We want to fix the leak in the bathroom faucet, but the blankety-blank thing won't go together like it should. Our sense of mastery, of skill, of knowledge is threatened. We wouldn't want our wife to know we can't fix a simple faucet; we're afraid she might think less of us.

A child who is frustrated at every turn by a father saying "No!" will often carry around a lump of anger inside, *rarely* expressing it directly at the father if expressing it at all, and he begins to fear his own anger. Even when the frustration and anger is unexpressed, the child may worry about being punished for having angry feelings.

Frustration, too, can set up the fear of failure, a fear most everyone experiences at one time or another. "This is just not working," we say to ourselves. "What if the whole idea just goes down the drain? What if I just can't do it?" Fear of failure is one of the most complicated and pervasive fears in our society; we'll deal with it in the following chapter on responses to our fears.

As we saw when we talked about power and fear, it is easy to be afraid when you are dependent on someone else for many of your needs. Dependency encourages fear. Inherently, dependence is not a bad thing. Healthy relationships are often called interdependent; that is, there is a balance of dependency. I depend on you for some of the things I need and you depend on me for some things you need. There is an equality that is felt by both partners and the gifts we give each other flow out of naturally being ourselves.

But dependence in a relationship is often out of balance and there are persons who go through life in a posture of dependency; they are not used to making their own decisions, to meeting many of their own needs, and they constantly look to others for responsibility and help.

This kind of dependency carries with it a sense of vulnerability, helplessness, and lack of control. If I feel this way, it can't help but feed all my fears. What would I do if my spouse left me? How will I ever carry off this job if the boss doesn't come with me? I'll never be able to finish this dress if Mom doesn't help me.

Children are the most obvious example of being dependent on others. The dependency that infants of all species feel for their parents is natural and healthy, up to a point. The size of children feeds this vulnerability and helplessness, as does their knowledge of the world and how they can affect it.

When I am small and sense my helplessness, it is easy to be afraid that my parent will leave me, that I won't be able to take care of myself on my own, that no one will love me. There is an important sense too, that what I do doesn't have too much influence, that what really matters—the big power and the big decisions—come from the top.

In healthy adults this extreme dependency passes and the experience of maturing is one of making our own decisions, making mistakes, doing things that we're afraid of and living with the consequences. For most of us those kinds of fear pass; for some, the failure to take responsibility and the fear stay.

One of the ways this kind of fear affects many of us is in the socio-political world. One of the frequent complaints people have about the world today is that what they do as individuals doesn't matter; their voices are not heard in the political process and, when you get right down to it, they don't have as much control as they would like to over their own survival. When there is a man thousands of miles away who you feel is not listening to you or responding to your needs, even though he has power over so many parts of your life—including plunging you into a global war—it is a situation practically designed to feed your insecurities. The less power people feel as individuals, the more helplessness they feel about controlling their own destinies, the more susceptible they are to being controlled by their fears. One of the most common responses to this kind of fear is to retreat into apathy.

Dependency and the fear of failure are linked together in a way. If I am too dependent on a boss, a teacher, or a spouse, I become, in some sense, obedient. I adopt their goals as my own or my goals grow out of what they want for me. Take, for instance, a domineering father who wants his son to attend Harvard

Business School. The boy, dependent on his father for money and approval, takes the goal on; perhaps he is not even aware it is not a decision of his own. Part of the fixation on his goal is the fear that he won't make it, that he will not only fail himself, but worse, he will fail his father. In his fearful state, it is hard to be fully open to other alternatives or other parts of his life. His performance in school is threatened by the fear that he won't make it. Beyond this dependency and adherence to what his father wants is freedom and openness to his own values and needs. Claiming that freedom for himself and following his own way is an act of courage.

Fear sometimes masquerades as guilt. Often our expression of guilt is a statement that "I am afraid that someone will find out about the real me, how bad I really am and when they do, they won't love me anymore." Wrapped up in guilt is a fear of discovery, being judged, rejected, humiliated, and finally, losing love, not only someone else's love but perhaps the love you have for yourself.

Part of the whole idea of guilt is giving the power of judging you to someone else—God, mother, husband, friend. They are the ones who are going to discover the rotten person we really are and pass judgment on us.

This mingling of fear and guilt was explored in a conversation I had with a friend, Andre Auw, a therapist in La Jolla, California:

> When I do something that makes me feel guilty I have a sense of disappointment in myself that I connected myself into something that I know is much less than I want to be. It's like I have let myself go and really made a mess of something and I know I'm better than that.
>
> It's fear. That's what it is. It's fear that comes as a result of some "should"—I don't always know where the should is coming from—but I experience a real fear of what's going to happen to me if I don't meet that should. That ties in with how my feelings about my own guilt have changed. I don't have as many shoulds as I used to and the ones I have are more my own than they are from other people or institutions. It's like some authority is telling me unless I do what I should I will suffer and I'm afraid of suffering. So that becomes a real weapon. The funny thing is, our

fear is sometimes so great that we never test it out to see if that great catastrophe will happen.

But sometimes guilt is really hard to get out of; for some it is a pattern of living. With clients of mine, what I try to do is guide them into experiences that formerly they might have felt guilty about but can now feel more okay about. I don't think guilt is something you can talk your way out of, but we all seem to try and do that. For me, it's more a question of experiencing things and feeling good about them instead of living in fear. Too many of us live in that powerless limbo and think we can't do anything about it. When we experience some things that make us feel a little strength to change our situation, a lot of that fear and guilt starts to go away.

In a sense, we give other people the right and the power to make us feel guilty. What I want to do is claim as much of that power as I can, as much as is rightfully mine. I want to take back the power that I've given to other people. What they think of me is not so important and I don't believe any more the things they say will happen to me. This sounds ideal to me—I'm not always this secure—but, generally, I'm just not afraid of what other people or institutions will do to me. If I'm not afraid of the punishment, I can't feel the guilt.

The more our own evaluations come from within ourselves, the freer we will be from guilt—and from fear.

Fritz Perls used to say guilt was 95 percent resentment; that whichever way our guilt was directed was a good place to look for resentment. He even had patients eliminate the use of the word guilt. Instead of saying: "I'm feeling guilty about being affectionate with this woman; my wife won't like it," Perls would have them say: "I resent my wife for disapproving of me when I'm doing something I want to." Of course the bottom line was to discover he was handing over that power to his wife, making it her decision, not taking his own responsibility and resenting her for it. To take our own responsibility, to be the seat of our own values, to be our own "quality control inspector" is to step away from the restrictions of fear.

Running through most of this, as far as I'm concerned, is a thread of insecurity. There is a nagging sense, when I am afraid, that I am not important. That what I am will not be enough, that what I want will not be valued, that what I say will not be listened to—all of this, though, springing from my own view of myself.

I am only one person. I may want something my wife and family don't. I may need something the telephone company doesn't think I should have. I want to go somewhere and two friends don't. Sometimes it feels as if I am only one among many and not important enough to step out and get what I want and need. This pervasive insecurity that so many of us bring to our adult lives affects not only our own view of ourself, but how we think others see us, the goals we set for ourselves and our attitudes about our future.

This is fertile ground for fear. The insecure person needs little real sense of harm to set up a persistent anxiety, no real threat to make him afraid. Just being alive in this big, complex world is enough, because inside he believes that, no matter what happens, he won't be able to cope. The slightest hint of disapproval from a boss or loved one is enough to throw him for a loop, afraid he will lose their approval and/or love. The smallest obstacle in his path is reason enough to sit down in the road and quit; he couldn't overcome it anyway.

To feel so insecure is to live in a world of dark shadows and strangers, of people who are not to be trusted and obstacles that cannot be overcome. It is to be paralyzed by fear.

There are many, many things in the development of a person that can lead to a sense of insecurity, too complex to develop here. Added to those factors in our individual development are a whole host of social influences that, in the words of one psychologist, "have raised mass cowardice to a new high."

My generation, as well as my father's, grew up with war. My childhood began with World War II and was followed with regional wars and tense national conflicts in rapid succession. There have been rapid and profound changes in our social system and in the things we value as a society. The family is changing drastically. The role of women is being questioned and changed, not only in a social sense, but in terms of their own view of themselves as a sex. All these changes and many more—the church, our government, our economic system—tend to enforce feelings of instability and insecurity.

The things that we have looked to and held onto for

meaning and stability are being changed so drastically that we don't recognize them. Your view of this, of course, depends on how heavily you have depended on institutions or structures. The point is, this instability outside ourselves, makes us easy prey to fears we harbor inside.

There is a tendency then to seek security, at any cost. We are like a drowning man thrashing around for a life preserver, or anything that floats. "Social security" is what we are looking for and we are looking outside ourselves, a frustrating and misleading search. We look to insurance, long-term contracts, retirement benefits, promises of happiness from instant gurus, and promises of life everlasting—as long as we can put our hope into anything except our own ability to get along in the world and make ourselves happy. There are many refuges, but eventually you find out that the only security worth having is the sureness of your faith in yourself.

PART TWO

Responses to Fear

CHAPTER 5

Fear and the individual

We have a choice. That is our uniqueness as humans; that is our blessing and our dilemma. We don't have to act out of our fear. We can consider our past without being trapped by it. We can weigh our hopes for the future. We can deliberate and act through our own wisdom, fear being a part of that wisdom.

In this and the next two chapters, we will look at our responses to fear—how it affects us as solitary individuals, how it enters into relationships with those closest to us, and how fear travels through our society and our world.

Let's take another brief look at our instant physical response to fear. Picture in your mind a primitive man, millions of years ago, lying in the warm afternoon sun in front of his hillside cave. He has just finished a food-gathering trip, has eaten, and is comfortable and secure. Suddenly there is a low growling sound in the brush nearby. Quickly his head comes up and he turns his face toward the sound, focusing his ears on the source of the sound. His brain has instantly sent his body an alarm signal: he is threatened.

Both his sympathetic and parasympathetic nervous systems rush signals to every part of his body and he becomes physically geared for a defense to the death or a quick getaway.

Adrenalin flashes into his bloodstream; more stored up energy! His pulse quickens, as does his respiration; more oxygen is needed and faster. His digestion stops; no time for that now. His blood is prepared to clot more readily in case of a wound. His sensory system is on a full-scale alert.

Cut to another scene thousands of generations later: a 35-year-old housewife is at home in her living room waiting for her husband to come home. Dinner is ready and the house is in order; nothing seems unusual except what she feels inside. She is about to tell her husband that she is going out tomorrow to look for a job, her first job since their marriage.

His car pulls into the driveway. Her pulse quickens and, unconsciously, she becomes more alert. Adrenalin pumps through her system as she paces nervously across the floor and back. All afternoon she has been troubled with a nervous stomach and she has smoked more than usual. Her brain has kept sending her body signals: What will he say about it? What if he really gets mad? What if he thinks I just want to get out of the house and away from him? Maybe I shouldn't talk about it yet. Maybe I don't need to do it after all.

Both the primitive man and the suburban housewife are in the grasp of fear; each, in his/her own way, is threatened. There is a real or imagined danger and the inclination is to defend or to hide.

The differences in the two situations are important in understanding our fears today. Though our chemical and involuntary reactions are the same, the sources of our fears are much more complex, vague, and harder to identify; in addition, we find it harder to identify and choose outlets for the energy and aggression fear may build up inside.

In our primitive ancestors, our defense alarm system kept us alive; it was sorely needed in the circumstances we were in. Now it seems, in a way, an anachronism. We are in a much more crowded and complex environment with different needs and different threats. Our gut reaction is the same, yet the real threats to our life and limb are rare. We now wander through the canyons and caves of New York City and an almost incessant barrage of danger signals attacks our nervous system; countless interchanges with people can be a threat to our emotional and/or physical security. All the while, our body tenses and relaxes, tenses and relaxes, tenses, tenses.

It is hardly a secret that the stresses of anxiety, fear and/or repressed anger are at the very least partially responsible for many of the diseases that are crippling and killing modern man such as heart disease, migraine headaches, ulcers, and asthma. One of the tragic effects of fear is that we are, in a sense, turning our energy inward and preying on ourselves.

An examination of some experiments scientists have carried out on animals shows us just how powerful and how persistent a force fear is and how we go on reacting to a fearful situation when we don't need to.

In the late 1940s a Yale professor named Neal Miller conducted a series of experiments to try to find out how persistent fear was as a learning experience. He tested a group of rats in a box with two compartments, one white with an electrified grid floor, the other black and safe from any shock.[1]

When the animals were shocked in the white compartment, they exhibited all the standard fearful reactions—squealing, running about aimlessly, defecation—but they quickly learned they could escape the shock by running through a door into the black compartment.

It didn't take many trials before they learned that the white side of the box was dangerous and the black side was safe. Whenever they were set in the white side, they frantically ran through the door to the back side, even without any shock at all. The symptoms of fear and the escape to the safety of the black side of the box persisted for hundreds of trials with no shock administered.

Miller decided to add an element. He rigged a small door

[1] Maggie Scarf, "The Anatomy of Fear," *New York Times Magazine*, June 16, 1974, p. 15.

between the two compartments and devised a wheel that the rats could turn to open the door. The rats quickly learned to rotate the wheel to escape the dangerous white side. Still no shock was needed to send the rats scurrying to the wheel to rotate it and escape. After relatively few trials, this behavior became less frantic and gradually took on the appearances of something the rats had done every day or would do naturally. They would move quickly to the wheel, turn it and scamper into the black box. The fear symptoms were gone, the shock—source of the fear—was gone, the panic was gone, but the persistent and durable behavior pattern remained. A relatively few painful experiences had made their mark and now the casual observer would find no clue that the animals' behavior was based on fear.

Another study at the University of Pennsylvania continued Miller's work, using dogs as subjects. A group of dogs was placed in one side of a box, divided in half by a tall divider. The box was artificially lighted and whenever the lights were dimmed, the dogs would automatically receive a mild electric shock. They escaped by leaping the divider into the other half of the box.

Soon the dogs learned that dimming lights meant pain was on the way and they became fearful and leapt the wall. As in the Miller study, the shocks were terminated and the dogs kept jumping whenever the lights would dim. And, as the rats, the dogs soon became more casual about their escape, yet they jumped higher and more quickly as they kept it up. They became more accomplished, in short, at escaping a learned signal of danger, even though the danger no longer existed.

Then the experimenters tried to countercondition the dogs by providing a shock when they came down on the previously safe side of the barrier. The lights would dim, with no shock, on the first side and the dogs would leap to the safe side, only to be shocked. *Ten of the thirteen dogs continued to leap, high and fast, through 100 trials!*

Two things struck me in particular about these experiments: that the animals' behavior was so persistent and endured through trials that numbered many, many more times the number of pain-producing experiences and that they would act on danger signals alone, without pain, to go back to a situation that pained them, over and over again, as much as the original experience. They were jumping out of fear and into pain. Interesting paradox, isn't it? Animals will take actions that cause them pain to avoid a pain they don't even know is there.

I'm sure it doesn't take much imagination or memory to see how we humans act in very similar ways. If there is a situation—a cocktail party, a blind date, a dance, or a person—a moody, aloof man, or an over-friendly, manipulating woman—that represents a danger signal, chances are we will avoid that side of the box and leap, by now quite casually, away to the other, safe side without even waiting to see if we get a shock.

Let's take a specific human example. A woman in her mid-twenties, who lived with a father she found cool, aloof, and demanding, now finds herself ending a brief marriage to a man with the same characteristics. The experience of wanting this man's love—her father's and her husband's—and not receiving it is too painful for her to endure and she has a strong need to escape the relationship. She leaves the marriage. Perhaps by now she has learned that men who seem unemotional, distant, and demanding will hurt her and she will adopt a behavior ensured to avoid that pain. Her relationships become briefer; she needs less and less time to determine that a man is too distant for her. Her ease at getting out of relationships becomes more and more apparent and, to an outside observer, almost casual. She jumps easily to the safety of either being alone or choosing a man who is not challenging, but will not satisfy her either. Being alone or being with a man she doesn't love is painful, but she chooses it instead of facing the pain rooted in her past. What she hasn't taken time enough to discover or summoned up courage enough to see is that perhaps any one of those brief relationships with men might have been satisfying and fulfilling, if she could have endured it, if she could have faced her own fear. By leaping consistently to the safe side, she may be depriving herself of what she really wants.

Perhaps you can think of an example out of your own life or that of a friend.

It might be argued that the woman in this example is safe from a painful experience she knows about first-hand and that she is making her own choice. While it is true that people acting this way can lead a relatively safe life (that is, they can avoid pain they have learned cues for), it is not a style I would choose for myself. There are several reasons why.

As we say in the chapter on definitions of fear, we have a tendency to generalize about our cues or danger signals. Thus as the boy Albert (in Chapter 2) learned quickly to be afraid of anything white and fuzzy, and the dogs became afraid anytime the lights dimmed, the woman in our example might learn, for instance, to tense up and avoid any man who doesn't immediately furnish her with good conversation, emotional support, and warmth. Each is taking the single, painful experience and predicting its recurrence in similar situations.

This kind of behavior limits our choices. When we are governed by a reaction to expected pain, we see the choices we can make on the safe side of the box or in a certain range of situations or types of people. This can happen in many areas of our lives—our professional life, our personal relations, including our friends and family, or our recreation and leisure time. The more our choices are limited, the more we become hemmed in and restricted from new experiences.

Take a budget officer for a medium-sized corporation, for example, who makes a decision involving quite a bit of money to buy new office equipment. The new equipment is late in arriving, costs more than expected and, it turns out, is very unpopular with the others in the office. All this earns the budget officer a severe reprimand from his boss. Stung by a harsh memo and the disapproval of his fellow employees, the man may not only avoid ordering anything new for the office but may tread awkwardly and cautiously into any professional decision he has to make. As a result his own satisfaction in his job is much less and he is less effective with the company.

Finally, there is the pain one jumps into. Acting out of fear, we surround ourselves with safeguards and eventually find we have built walls around ourselves. New experiences, unusual people, challenging situations, big decisions, and any kind of change paralyze us. We become inactive and indecisive. Eventually spontaneity and discovery elude us and we are into a routine that is safe but lifeless.

In each of the examples above, we have seen a person or other animals respond to a fear that was learned. There was an initial painful experience from a neutral or even pleasant environment or other person. The pain was repeated. From that time on, the response was based on the early learning and in anticipation of pain.

This expectation of punishment is one of the most powerful currents in the fear that flows through our lives. It begins in our infancy and follows us to the grave. But, again, our choice can be to unlearn behaviors that restrict us and learn new things about ourselves and the people around us that may bring pleasure instead of pain.

We are unconsciously governed by attitudes and values we acquire in the earliest years of our life and in the process of growing and maturing we are constantly testing and correcting or underlining those most basic parts of ourselves. We learn to distinguish between things we have been punished for as children and things that society will punish us for as adults. Perhaps we will make our own choices about eating candy, or not washing, or singing out loud, or having sex; or maybe childhood prohibitions will continue to haunt us.

For some, there are many experiences in the world that are considered "no-no's" and any time a person approaches that behavior which is considered evil, hence punishable, he or she becomes fearful, expecting punishment. This is most often unconscious and powerful. The symptoms of fear are evident and so is the primitive response we've read about—to retreat, to flee, to hide.

It follows that the more judgments and standards and inhibitions a person has had handed down during the years he or she is most vulnerable to those, the more definitions of good and evil there are in his or her world. There are more chances to be wrong, to be "a bad kid," whether it is in the eyes of God, father, teacher, commanding officer, foreman, or any other authority. There are more possibilities to be wrapped in a web of fear.

It is hard to imagine anyone without innumerable judgments and standards of what is good and bad in the world; indeed this formation of values is one of the most important parts of our upbringing and learning. But I have experienced all too many people who are so bogged down with the legacy of others' judgments that they have no sense of what their own are and will not act out of a fear of having someone somewhere condemn them. Without a base of security about themselves and a sense of personal power, they have not tested their own view of the world and formed their own values.

Henry Miller, in an essay (and a book) called *The Wisdom of the Heart*, wrote about this position some of us find ourselves in:

> In his present fearsome state man seems to have but one attitude, *escape*, wherein he is fixed as in a nightmare. Not only does he refuse to accept his fears, but worse, he *fears* his fears. Everything seems infinitely worse than it is, says [E. Graham] Howe, "just because we are trying to escape." This is the very Paradise of Neurosis, a glue of fear and anxiety, in which, unless we are willing to rescue ourselves, we may stick forever. To imagine that we are going to be saved by outside intervention, whether in the shape of an analyst, a dictator, a savior or even a God, is sheer folly. There are not enough lifeboats to go around, and anyway, as the author points out, what is needed more than lifeboats is lighthouses. A fuller, clearer vision—not more safety appliances.[2]

That kind of "glue of fear and anxiety" seeps around all of us at one time or another. Let's look at some other responses to fear, from people in varying stations in life.

Author Hugh Prather wrote in his book, *Notes to Myself*:

> There may be a natural, healthy kind of fear, but the kind of fear I don't like and want not to obey is the fear that urges me to act contrary to my own feelings or to act before I know what my feelings are. It is usually a fear of displeasing other people. It is most often a fear of not doing what I (too quickly) assume others expect. I feel smaller, weaker and less a person after I have acted out of this kind of fear. I want to be aware of what others expect but not despotized by it. If I reflexively choose the opposite of what they expect I am still being controlled. What I want is to act out of love and respect for myself.[3]

I was struck by the fact that some of Prather's fear resulted from giving up power to others *and* by his awareness that he did not have to act out of that fear.

---

[2] Henry Miller, *The Wisdom of the Heart*, p. 35. Copyright 1941 by New Directions Publishing Corporation. Reprinted by permission of New Directions Publishing Corporation.

[3] Hugh Prather, *Notes to Myself* (Moab, Utah: Real People Press, 1970).

A counselor at a Canadian college, Chris Ross, wrote this response when I asked him to write about his fear:

> The first flicker of fear comes into my mind . . . there is an instant alarm inside when I recognize something that could hurt me. It could be seeing my car start to slide across an icy road or realizing that my father dislikes what I just said. A dull sensation grows behind my eyes. I become aware that other parts of my body are already changing. It feels as if my blood is flaming or draining away and my limbs feel vibrant and unsteady. My heart quakes and my chest seems to sink. My fear sinks down and the stomach and abdomen becomes the focus of the storm as muscles turn against each other.
>
> Then, it seems, *one of the two things can happen.* If my eyes and ears declare that the signal from outside was a *false alarm*, the intensity decreases, leaving a somewhat meandering knot of tension. This may linger for some time and in this state I feel vulnerable to danger in the surroundings or from someone whom I feel may hurt me. I sometimes try and distract myself with cigarettes, drinks, or nervous munching.
>
> But if eyes and ears confirm the dangers, the muscles in the center of my body gnash on, tighter and tighter. For protection I may fold my arms over my stomach or put my hands between my legs to ally the quaking that has started in my balls and rectum. Or else I just try and contract my body into as small a ball of fear as possible.
>
> My attention has become riveted on the exact source of fear in the surroundings. My mind is running at an accelerated rate, working through a thousand alternatives. I may seize one. It doesn't work. I can't steer the car out of the skid! My God, my dad will see how weak I am and throw me to the ground! So I search out other actions.
>
> When my fear is of another person, I may gain temporary respite by realizing: I am afraid. I am still me. This is happening to me but it is only part of me. If I am feeling strong I may own my fear and tell the other person. But my voice will be trembling, the sound strained as I try to control those shaky insides.
>
> Once I get some kind of reaction, I feel better. It's not perfect but at least I have something to work on for a while. My self has been preserved; I am not lost. I can move on.

There is not only a real sense of the physical responses to fear but a realization of how they might be triggered by a threat of physical danger or an exchange with his father. And in reading it you can see Chris' realization that his power and sense of himself slowly returns, that he has responded to a part of himself, and by testing the situation, he can move toward a kind of personal wholeness.

Columnist Stewart Alsop takes us into the consciousness of a man who knows he is dying and tells us a little about his fear. This is from *Stay of Execution: A Sort of Memoir.*

> A man can't be afraid all the time. No doubt if you were told that you were to die in three hours, you would spend those three hours being afraid of death. But when death is due to occur at some time in the fairly near but indefinite future—in a few months, or a year, or two years, or maybe even later—it is possible to forget about death for many hours at a time.
>
> Most people have experienced the fear of death at one time or another—in combat, or at the moment of collision on a highway, or in the air, when something serious has gone wrong. That kind of fear is sudden and sharp, with familiar symptoms— the quickened pulse rate, the sweating of the palms. This was different. It was always present, like a kind of background music. Sometimes it receded almost into inaudibility, and then sometimes it would come blaring back, accompanied by a sense of incredulity. "My God, I really *do* have cancer, and I really am going to die." [4]

The fear of death, as Alsop says, is something most of us avoid, put off to the last minute, so to speak. But it can be called to the foreground quickly; anyone who has undergone a serious operation has probably "entertained" the fear of death for a while.

There are other responses to fear. In his book *Anatomy of Courage*, Lord Moran examined the behavior of English soldiers in combat. In this section he measures fear against a man's self-respect:

> There are signals of personal defeat which are like red lamps on broken roads, to these we must pay heed. I grew anxious when a man's speech began to betray him; when he was full of

---

[4] From *Stay of Execution*, by Stewart Alsop. Copyright © 1973 by J. B. Lippincott Company. Reprinted by permission of J. B. Lippincott Company and The Estate of the Author.

windy talk of what the Boche had done in the new sector the battalion was taking over, of some new gas. It was always about something which was going to happen; the wretched fellow must have known the mess would muzzle him if it could, but he seemed driven by some inner force to chatter incessantly of every calamity that could conceivably come to pass. It was as if he had come to terms with the devil himself, that if he could make others as windy, his life would be spared. How full of apprehension the fellow was; death came to him daily in a hundred shapes. This was fear in its infancy. It was a bad sign, for when a man talked like that, his self-respect was going, and the battle was already half lost. It was just a matter of time. Such a man did the battalion no good for the disease was infectious; I was glad to get him away.

But sometimes the shadow of fear drove men in just the opposite direction, into sheer recklessness. And yet this recklessness meant different things in different men. Sometimes it was only an act of self-discipline whereby some too sensitive soul hoped to school himself or test his self-control. We had no need to bother about such a man; he would cast out the demon for himself before it devoured him; he would win through; his self-respect was intact.[5]

Perhaps there are people in your life who "chatter incessantly of every calamity that could conceivably come to pass." Maybe, if they're a parent or a friend, they are always warning you of the terrible things the world and other people can bring down on you. If they would talk more openly, you would see that their words are based on their own fear of the world and their warnings are reflections of scenes of pain and punishment that pass through their own fantasies.

Just as there are thousands of different things that pass through our minds that can make us afraid, there are thousands of different responses we each can have to that fear. We have only explored a few here.

Remember, that the first, most basic response is to flee and conceal yourself; of course, there are many ways to do that without running into your cave. We hide ourselves all the time.

[5] Lord Moran, *Churchill: Taken from the Diaries of Lord Moran.* Copyright © Trustees of Lord Moran. Nutley Publications Ltd., 1966; reprinted by permission of Houghton Mifflin Company.

We sometimes conceal true responses to people, statements, and things we absolutely dislike, *and* we hide responses to things that excite us as well.

Admitting your fear, bringing it out into the open to stand the test of reason and a different reality, is a difficult thing for most of us. Alan Paton, the South African who wrote *Cry the Beloved Country*, touched this point in a recent essay:

> . . . I am searching for an explanation of the fact that under some circumstances men readily admit fear and under other circumstances do not. I assume that readiness to admit fear is part of a general readiness to look at the world as it is and therefore at oneself as one is, while unwillingness to admit fear may be a strong element in self-esteem. One does not readily admit to a fear of which one is ashamed.[6]

Yet fear thrives on the very things it urges us to do—conceal ourselves, flee. It is as if fear is a self-supporting organism that produces and nurtures the conditions that it needs to survive. The more it is covered and kept from the light, the bigger it grows and the more powerful its hold on us becomes.

Fear is, as Paton says, a "wretched determinant of conduct. There is nothing more pitiable than a human being whose conduct is largely determined by fear." [7]

Yet when we use our own awareness and take hold of our own personal power (which most of us have in a more ready supply than we are willing to use), we can make choices that use fear in a more positive way. I want to deal with this more thoroughly in later chapters, but there are two basic points we have touched on here that I want to underline.

Some writers and psychologists have said that fear is the root of art, that man creates out of the fear that he will pass through his life and leave no visible trace behind. Hermann Hesse makes the point beautifully in this passage from *Narcissus and Goldmund*:

> He [Goldmund] thought that fear of death was perhaps the root of all art, perhaps also of all things of the mind. We fear death, we shudder at life's instability, we grieve to see the flowers

---

[6] Alan Paton, "The Challenge of Fear," *Saturday Review*, September 9, 1967, p. 20.
[7] Ibid., p. 21.

wilt again and again, and the leaves fall, and in our hearts we know that we, too, are transitory and will soon disappear. When artists create pictures and thinkers search for laws and formulate thoughts, it is in order to salvage something from the great dance of death, to make something that lasts longer than we do.[8]

Does our creativity spring from a deep dread of the nothingness that awaits us? Do we sing, paint, dance, sculpt, and write to fill a space and time that we are only passing through, to leave some imprint? Is this one of the responses we have to one of our most powerful and primitive emotions?

If we find this to be true then perhaps we can look at our fear in a different light; we can, if we are aware and can summon this courage, use our fears as a springboard to a more fulfilling life.

Finally, several times during this chapter there has been reference to fears coming out of a part of a person, that responses to fear are not based in unity or wholeness.

There are two sides to this. My own experience is that I can be afraid, of a person, for instance, and later find that only a part of my personality was threatened in some way. My masculine self was threatened or the part of me that wants to know more than others was shaken. When I can see this and see that I am not listening and responding to the rest of me, I can deal much more easily with my fear. I am made up of many parts and in most cases, fear touches only one or a few of these.

The other side follows; as Hugh Prather puts it: "Fear is often an indication I am avoiding myself." If there is something I am afraid of, perhaps it is because there is a part of my personality I am unwilling to expose, much less admit to myself. If I avoid gentleness and intimacy in another, maybe it's because I am afraid it would be weak and not masculine to admit that I too felt gentle and tender and vulnerable.

There are different parts of our personality, just as there are many different small towns in a circle we would draw on a map. Sometimes it is more comfortable to stay at home in the stance

---

[8] Reprinted with the permission of Peter Owen, London and Farrar, Straus & Giroux, Inc. from *Narcissus and Goldmund* by Hermann Hesse, translated by Ursule Molinaro, copyright © 1968 by Farrar, Straus & Giroux, Inc.

and in the roles that we are used to and from which we are accustomed to getting our support. To travel to those other parts would be a new experience, one that might change things, and that's scary.

But to move to and embrace the estranged parts of our own person is to move to unity, wholeness, a rounding out of all that we are and can be. On that journey, our fears can be the directional signs.

CHAPTER 6

Fear between us

I am afraid to be who I am with you.

If there were one sentence that could summarize this entire chapter, that would be it. I am afraid to be judged by you, I am afraid you will reject me. I am afraid you will say bad things about me. I am afraid you will hurt me. I am afraid, if I really am myself, you won't love me—and I need your love so badly that I will play the roles you expect me to play and be the person that pleases you, even though I lose myself in the process.

This inner dialogue plays, over and over again, through the minds and hearts of people in a close relationship. In many, it moves them though they aren't aware of it. Others catch glimpses of how they are living their life, but don't want to see that picture fully. They are too afraid to see themselves. Still others play the tape to themselves openly and resent their partners and the way they are together.

This is one of the typical ways that fear winds its ugly barbed-wire fence between two individuals who both want and fear intimacy.

Volumes have been written about couples and intimacy; it is not the purpose of this chapter to try and cover that ground, worthwhile as it is. Rather, I want to make some important points about how fear leads us to certain responses in close relationships. Friend to friend, parent to child, wife to husband, lover to lover—these are some of the relationships I think about in this context; basically it is a one-to-one relationship that we can loosely call a couple.

The idea of really being *with* another person is very important. It may sound very basic to say that, but many persons within couples today are finding it very confusing and painful, as well as satisfying, to be fully with another. They are struggling with the concept and the reality of interdependence, compromise, expectations, demands, freedom, and the growth of themselves as individuals as it relates to the growth of the couple.

All this is changing. It does not mean today what it meant yesterday to be a couple. Rules have gone out the window. Values have changed. What society will allow without condemnation has changed. In a way, for many couples, there are no ground rules and when they come together they often find themselves in the position of breaking new ground in many ways in which they relate to each other. They are in a real way exploring new ways of being couples and when you are making those kinds of explorations, it can be scary. There is a tendency to fall back onto old roles and old ways of behaving to gain some security. That struggle, of wanting to move ahead to new kinds of relationships and feeling the tugs of security and comfort in old ways of relating, is one area where fear plays a strong hand.

This new "coupleness" is apparent not only with young people in a man-woman relationship, but with older couples, a teacher and a student, a father or mother and their son or daughter, and between friends of either sex. In each case, there is the recognition that each of the partners is a separate and distinct individual and has needs and fears and ways of behaving that are unique. In some cases these may match up with a partner's needs and behaviors; often the needs are separate and taken care of by themselves and sometimes they are in direct conflict with what the partner wants.

What has taken place most often in the past is that there was one partner—the woman, the child, the student, the more dependent friend—who was recognized as subordinate. That person's needs were met in the context of a bigger picture, that the man, parent, teacher, or more dominant friend had more important needs and his or her behavior guided the course of the relationship.

Women's liberation, though it conjures up too many stereotypes, offers a ready example. Remember though, that while "a liberated woman" in a couple serves as this example, the same general thing is true of others in one-to-one relationships. Many, many women that I know (and of course women we have all read about) are no longer—to put it too simply—accepting the place in the world that others had figured out for them.

As the individual woman struggles to find a new picture of herself, to realize her own potential, to find out new ways of relating to those close to her and to society, time and time again she runs up against her relationship to the person closest to her. If this is a man, she is often continually teased back, forced back, lured back into ways of relating that they are both more used to and that society still recognizes as the norm. Not only does her partner apply pressure, there is pressure from within to stop all this disruptive and frightening behavior.

The woman is going to find herself and on this new journey, with new rules and new values, it is possible that her path will take her away from a partner. In many couples, the same thing is going on in the man. He, too, is rejecting old roles and ways of being in the world. All of this change includes, of course, the way they relate to each other and what they expect.

Again, the picture is of the struggle of two individuals wanting very much to "become themselves" set against their wants to be in an intimate relationship with another and deal with the dependencies and compromises that go along with any relationship.

I think about two very good friends, a man and a woman who have been married for several years. They seem to function well as a couple; they are intimate yet they maintain a strong sense of separate identity. Last winter Anne became restless with what she was doing and was drawn to a school and a group of people in the East. At the same time Bill, who had been writing and consulting in California, where they lived, was offered a teaching post in Arizona.

They love each other and they want to be together. Anne's restlessness and feelings of wanting to do something on her own were acknowledged. Bill's desire to teach and have a more secure source of income was acknowledged. In an "old" way of being a couple, the decision would have been made going in—they would have both gone to Arizona and the new teaching job.

As it was, Anne went to Boston for the fall term and Bill took the teaching job in Arizona—a frightening decision to make in many ways. Yet the closeness of their relationship is based on the separateness of the two individuals. It is when that conflict of separateness and togetherness is resolved and two people can meet recognizing each other's wholeness that true intimacy can exist.

It is against this backdrop, a very important one, that I want to explore fear in one-to-one relationships. It may seem to some a paradox but I maintain that I cannot achieve true intimacy with you unless I acknowledge and act on my own separate identity and you do the same. We must meet recognizing each other's wholeness, otherwise there is an inequality that undermines a genuine coming together of all facets of two persons.

If I give up power to you, I cannot love you. If I am afraid of you, I cannot love you. As St. John says, "Perfect love casteth out fear";[1] and fear robs a relationship of love. Fear is the doorway that must be walked through in order to share yourself with another in love and to commit yourself to the nourishment of another person.

But it is our nature to change. People change, relationships change, and the world changes around us all the while. So that even as we walk through one fear, as we summon up the courage to make some change in ourselves or our relationship, another doorway is before us. Another opportunity, another challenge presents itself. It is a risk, as it is an invitation.

[1] John, 4:8.

The pace of social change in our age is such that a husband and wife are faced with a dizzying list of challenges and issues within their relationship—issues that in the past have taken whole generations, or several of them, to work their way into our lives. Sex before marriage, the liberation of women, easily available and effective birth control, abortion, more frequent divorce, swapping of sexual partners, living together unmarried, higher expectations of a marriage, the allowance of relationships outside the couple—all of these questions or issues or possibilities, however you regard them, now present themselves to couples. A century ago a husband and wife (surely legally married) may have been presented or challenged with one or two similarly weighty issues in the lifetime of their relationship. A couple today may deal with all of them.

Each of these current issues is set against the backdrop of two human beings getting together to have a happy, lasting relationship. There are problems enough in that. Each of these issues mentioned present choices; many are personal frontiers or challenges. They are new doorways to walk through or a stop sign urging entrenchment or retreat. Potentially, they are each sources of fear.

At the same time these issues present themselves to couples, individuals are facing them within themselves, on top of whatever growth pains they are going through that don't have to do with relationships!

Let me try and state this more simply. I am growing as a separate person and facing my own challenges. I also see issues that are alive and current with me that have to do with relationships, whether I happen to be in one or not. I am faced with those questions as well. Then too, if you and I are together I must deal with the realities of us, of your growth and fears and how we come together.

All of this can seem terribly weighty and complicated. At times, I've experienced it that way and it seems easy to be overwhelmed by it. But in at least an equal number of cases, I have felt it exciting and joyous. When an experience or a relationship demands my full measure, I know meeting it with my full self will provide all the satisfaction I ask for.

Fear is the enemy of that full presentation. To the extent

that I am afraid I defend myself—from strangers, my family, even you, the person I am *with* the most. As I defend myself, there are parts of me that I don't fully know; how could you possibly know them? And if you don't know those parts of me, how could you love me?

For my book *How Do You Feel? A Guide to Your Emotions*, I wrote in a personal way about this feeling of being afraid and defended. I think it's pertinent here.

> Being defensive is a very important concept to me. I see a lot of people for whom it is a way of life; it's their way of relating to the world. In me, it has an awful lot to do with my growth. I don't think I can grow and be open to change when I am being protective.
>
> When I am defensive I am afraid. It could be afraid of being hurt, rejected or unloved. Sometimes I recognize myself saying, "Oh, oh, someone is about to discover something bad in me. They're about to find out something I don't want them to know." There is a feeling of girding myself, of setting up smokescreens and barriers to protect that sore spot.
>
> I get quiet and withdrawn. I avoid contact with people and if I do talk, I will try to manipulate the conversation around to unimportant matters. The closer someone gets in conversation to the weak or evil thing I'm protecting, the higher I build the barriers, the more veiled I become.
>
> There are certain kinds of people who will make me feel defensive and withdrawn. Someone who seems certain about everything has that effect on me; someone who is sure of where he is and where he's going, know's what's right and wrong with the world and seems like he knows what's right and wrong for me. Someone like that can make me unsure of myself and protective of the things I think he will judge. Also I am defensive if I'm with someone who has much higher standards than I do and he or she expects me to live up to them . . . and I think I have to live up to them too. In those cases, it often feels like I want the other person's praise and that praise is withheld until I come up to their standards. I don't know why I give all that power to someone else.
>
> I seem to get the most defensive when I think something I have done is "bad." The judgment as to what is bad is a judgment of mine as well as others around me. It cuts the most when someone else's judgment of me agrees with my own bad impression of myself. I seem very susceptible to a "bad boy" thing. I can

get pouty and withdraw just like a bad boy would. When I get that way or get an impression of someone reacting to me in that way, I quickly blame them for being judgmental and not understanding me. I begin to feel misunderstood, unloved, unknown, and alone.

There are particular things in my life that I tend to judge myself for and so feel sensitive about . . . being over-sexual, selfish, indecisive, cool, aloof, and critical. When someone taps into one of those areas I don't like about myself, I can get very defensive, tight as a drum. That seems to be a case of me protecting an "evil truth" in myself.

Perhaps the way out of that is through self-acceptance. Today I can see clearly and say to myself that I am not a bad person and even those bad traits I think I have are not present in me all the time. Though sometimes I am aloof, critical and cool, there are at least an equal number of times when I am really present with people, accepting, affectionate, and warm. Why can't I see that in myself more clearly and allow my "lapses." Must I be perfect?

An important part of this has to do with two images . . . of a core of myself and a shell. When I feel the central core of myself, when I know what I'm about and can present that to the situation, I rarely have a need to defend. I feel myself "filled out" in a sense and there is nothing to hide. Another way to feel, perhaps the opposite, is to sense that I am just a shell, thinly disguising an empty person inside. My core has vanished . . . I don't know myself or have any faith in what's inside of me. That shell is crusty, hard and brittle; surely I must protect myself because the inside is dark and vacuous. I am very vulnerable.[2]

You can see how much a part of this statement has to do with self-image, how much my positive or negative view of myself influences my presentation of myself to another person. I can't expect another to love me—and deep down I know they won't—until I love myself enough to offer the varied good and bad parts of me to the relationship.

So what are we afraid of? What ogre lies around the corner waiting to gobble up the tender parts of our personage that we bring out into the open?

[2] John T. Wood, *How Do You Feel? A Guide to Your Emotions* (Englewood Cliffs, N.J.: Prentice-Hall, Inc., 1974), pp. 74–76.

Failure, for one thing. We are afraid to present, to give it all we've got because we're afraid it won't be enough.

"Why are we afraid of failure?", Robert Schuller asks in his book, *Self-Love: The Dynamic Force of Success.*

> We fearfully believe that our friends will forsake us if we fail. We're afraid we will lose all self-respect if that should happen. In trying to spare our self-love from the wounds of humiliation, we actually surrender to the dominating fear of failure to restrain us from plunging into what might be called a humiliating experience. The fear of failure, then, is a self-contrived defense mechanism subconsciously fabricated to shelter our insecure self-love from possible embarrassment.[3]

So we enter into a relationship, afraid that who we are won't do it. And sure enough, it doesn't. For in not overcoming our fear enough to offer parts of ourself to the relationship, we set up our own failure. It is what some counselors call a "self-fulfilling prophecy." In order to protect ourselves from failure, we hold back and proceed with caution, if at all. This gives another person little to love and saps the relationship of energy. Gripped by the fear of failing, we fail.

Failure and the fear of failure can probably be best understood and focused on in an interpersonal context. It is here, person-to-person, that there is a high-risk, high-reward situation; it is down to the essence of who we are and some of our fondest hopes for ourselves. If we "succeed" in an intimate relationship, we can "achieve" a lasting love, a sense of security, a home, a loving family, a whole way of life that we have dreamed about. Especially in our society, "success" is an important part of how you see yourself and how others see you. So it follows that your love of self, we have been taught, is tied up with your "success" or your "failure." Success in a couple or a marriage is highly valued.

The catch is that success and failure are most often thought of and described in the eyes of others—your mother, teacher, boss, mate, the neighbors, your peers. When we see how it is largely "others" outside ourself who determine our success and

---

[3] Robert H. Schuller, *Self-Love: The Dynamic Force of Success* (New York: Hawthorn Books, 1969), p. 124.

failure and how so much loss of esteem and value are attached to failure, it is easy to see why many of us are bound up with the fear of failing.

If we examine some basic research about the fear of failure, we can see some of the ways we respond to that fear and how it affects our ability or willingness to be intimate.

In a book called *Fear of Failure*, Robert Birney, Harvey Burdick, and Richard Teevan point out that a person reacts to cues that tell him he is about to fail.[4] He anticipates failing, but since the failure hasn't happened yet, he has a chance to avoid it. Afraid of failing, he will engage in various defensive behaviors that will, while they serve his fear, also set up his failure. The greater the fear, the greater the defense.

The authors look at three basic kinds of fear and define various responses to those. The three kinds of fear are (1) a reduction of self-estimation; (2) a non-ego punishment; and, (3) a loss in social value.

In a general way, these observations might apply to a guy you know in the Tuesday night bowling league or to a vice-president at the bank. Here we look at the findings in the context of a person-to-person relationship and how it applies to intimacy. In the first area, a person is afraid his opinion of himself will be drastically lowered by not achieving what he has set out to do. But remember, his own opinion of himself, especially if he is insecure, is closely tied up with how he thinks others see him.

One of the things a person might do to defend against this lesser view of himself is avoid any precise picture he has of himself. He may not take the time to find out about himself and construct any clear-cut picture of who he is; as long as this self-estimate is vague, it is unclear whether his performance meets his expectations or not.

A person might lower her own standards to keep from failing. In a relationship with a man, for instance, a woman might "settle" for a partner who is not her equal and maintain a relationship that is below the standards she had set for herself

---

[4] Robert C. Birney, Harvey Burdick, and Richard Teevan, *Fear of Failure* (New York: Van Nostrand Reinhold, 1969).

earlier. A similar defense would be to prefer situations or relationships that are easy—that is, without much conflict and/or challenge. If the task or the relationship is easy, chances for failure are lessened.

A man might prefer isolation or privacy. The less the number of relationships he starts, the less contact he makes with people, the smaller his chances for failure are.

Another defensive behavior is the rejection of responsibility. If a wife, for example, leaves all decisions up to her husband regarding their finances, or their home, or how they will make love, she is giving away any chance she has to make her own choices and fail.

When situations or exchanges are inappropriately seen as games or are treated light-heartedly, this can be a defense against failure, too. Not that humor and games aren't part of life, but a continual shucking off of a serious matter into fun and games is not facing up to real issues and conflicts. An example might be a man and a woman who continually throw verbal darts back and forth at each other, laughing all the while, and when confronted claim: "I was only kidding."

If a person continually reduces the importance of matters, he is likely avoiding failure. By losing interest, not trying, or saying, "Ah, this isn't worth it," a man signals that he is not going to give you his full effort and risk failing. A woman invites her husband to learn a new craft hobby or take tennis lessons, for instance. After a half-hearted attempt in one class, she is met with the comment: "This is a drag. Learning to throw pots is a waste of time." He may simply be afraid of failing.

One other defensive behavior is to misjudge or forget mistakes made in the past. If we can see ourselves in the best possible light and only look at our best performances, how could we have failed? In a relationship, this might take the form of forgetting or remembering incorrectly something you did to hurt or disappoint your partner. "I didn't say that; I couldn't have done that. I'm not that bad."

All of these defenses are, in a sense, a smokescreen in front of who a person really is. The greater the smoke, the less we know, the less there is to love. The more defenses, the less trust there is, and that leaves less and less room for intimacy.

The fear of failing related to an expectation of punishment is complex. We have seen that the fear of punishment is one of the most powerful of our motivations and that some of us, humans and animals alike, will "lose face" in our own eyes and in the eyes of others to avoid punishment. We will endure the punishment of failing to avoid what we consider a greater punishment.

There are many ways to punish a person you're close to; the withholding of love may be, at the same time, the most common and the most feared. It may be that a wife will forego her own values and goals—that she will risk failure as her own person—to avoid the punishment her husband might give her by withholding his love.

Similarly, a child will give up things he is drawn to and that give him pleasure, if he expects a heavy punishment from his parents.

If you imagine yourself in a situation from which you cannot escape and a punishment looms over your head, there may be a different reaction. A boy is expected to achieve in school, for instance, or be subject to certain punishment at home. The fear of being punished by his parents becomes greater than any fear he has of failing in his own eyes or those of his classmates at school, so he gives his school work his best try and takes his chances on failing. There is an important if. The boy must sense a reasonable chance of succeeding, of achieving the goals his parents have set for him, or he is liable to resign himself to the punishment and save the energy of trying.

In any case, his actions are based on the goals set by someone else and his behavior is a defense against punishment. If he is defending himself, it is hard for him to love.

The third area Birney, Burdick, and Teevan discussed was defensive behavior to protect against a loss in social value. To protect your opinion of me, I might tell you about all the things I've succeeded at or invite you to witness something I'm doing when there is a good chance I'll look good.

A man might constantly make excuses; if his reasons for not succeeding are good enough, he is protected from a harsh judgment from his peers.

A woman might make, and come to believe, statements

about herself that indicate low aspirations and low expectations. If she doesn't want much or expect too much from her marriage, for instance, she is not left open to criticism that she hasn't gotten it. To let others know what you want is to make yourself vulnerable, but that vulnerability is the same quality that lets them in on the real person you are.

Our fear of failing is a set-up. We are set up to respond in a way that keeps part of us in reserve. We didn't give it all we had, we can make excuses, we played at it, we didn't really want it in the first place—or whatever defense we choose to use. What they all mean is that we chose to hold back because of fear. Holding back and not giving what you are to an experience, a goal you have set for yourself, or a relationship is the antithesis of satisfaction and joy.

Not only do we burden ourselves with these fears, which stand in our way of intimacy, but we transfer them to those close to us. Children take on the fears of their parents, students learn to be afraid as are their teachers, and marriage partners fear the things their spouses are afraid of. If someone I care about and respect is afraid of something, that's good enough reason for me to fear it too. Besides that, if I am afraid of something and can keep my partner afraid of it too, that will shelter my fear.

I know a woman who is deathly afraid of exploring her own sexuality. She is afraid to let go and explore, to lose control, to experience some new ways of being with her husband. If she can keep a tight rein on that, which includes closing down any experimenting her husband might want, she will not have to face her own fears. If her husband should start to explore his own sexual options and want more variety in their sex life, it would draw her in to the very thing she's afraid of. So we transfer our fears and then seek to keep that relationship within the bounds we have set for ourselves.

Another reaction to fear in a close relationship is to discount the things someone close to you is afraid of. This happens between man and woman and parent and child most frequently. "Don't be silly. There's nothing to be afraid of." That kind of response, to a genuine expression in another, is a put-down.

One National Institute of Mental Health study found that parents are disturbed when they find their children are afraid; it bothers fathers to know that their boys are frightened, "weak," and "unmanly." It means to the fathers that they have somehow failed in bringing up a brave boy. "What are you afraid of? Don't be a sissy." Those words hammer home a denial of part of a person and, further, mean that such revelations in the future will be unwelcome.

Fears are hard to reveal. We subject ourselves to shame and ridicule and make ourselves vulnerable to others when we admit that we are afraid. To be afraid of being afraid is a double coat, a sticky bind of fear and shame that is doubly hard to get out of.

What we need, to disclose our fears, is an environment that is safe for disclosure, where feelings won't be denied or scoffed at. If I am to tell you my fears I can't be afraid of you. And I will be much better able to handle my own fears when I don't need to hide the fact that I'm frightened.

Fear in a personal relationship also has a lot to do with control. To the extent that a man is afraid of where a relationship will lead, if it takes its natural course, he will try to control it. If he is afraid of his own impulses—sexual, aggressive, or other—he will try to control them. If he is afraid of what his partner will do, or his child, he will try and chart a course that will subtly lead through calm waters, waters where he is sure of himself.

When a person manipulates, it is out of fear of what will happen if he or she doesn't. In this situation, the person controlled is susceptible to fear as well as the person doing the controlling. A woman thoroughly dominated by her husband operates out of the fear of what he'll do to her if she doesn't make him happy. The husband worries about what would happen if he ever let his wife have her own reins.

From either side of the relationship, fear is a barrier to intimacy. Where there is control and power given from one person to another, there is in some degree a master-slave relationship and that inequality leaves little room for real openness or trust.

It is hard to over-emphasize just how much this control springing from fear means. To me, this kind of control, manipulation, or seizing of power is the opposite of love. It is so easy in a relationship, and so subtle, to start taking responsibility for another person and guide and shape the relationship into what one half of it wants.

The commitment in a loving relationship is to nourish another and to reveal yourself. By nourishing someone else, it may mean that your partner will grow in directions you don't want him or her to. By revealing yourself you are giving away power you might gain by withholding feelings or information.

The fear, then, of giving up power, of revealing one's self, and of providing nourishment for another's growth, although it is real and readily understandable, works to undermine the very intimacy all of us want so badly.

Underlying all of this discussion of fear and intimacy is the whole area of being aware of our feelings. It continues to amaze me how unaware we are of our emotions, how naive we are about how much they influence our day-to-day lives and how we underestimate their power.

We have grown up and learned how to take care of ourselves physically—most of us can provide food, clothing, and shelter for ourselves and we can get around in the world; most of us can express ideas and discuss events we see and read about; yet, on the whole, we know relatively little about the expression of emotions between two human beings. We leave that up to the experts, the "shrinks." Most of us find it awkward, embarrassing, and dreadfully risky to express an honest, direct feeling we have for someone else or about ourselves.

What does this vacuum in our development lead to? Because we know so little of our emotions and what to do with them, it is much easier for them to control us than for us to have any kind of control over them. Because we are so unaware of our feelings and don't have a good vocabulary for expressing them, we are afraid of them. Our own emotions! We are particularly afraid of strong feelings; we are terrified of negative feelings.

Yet the awareness and revelation of emotions—particularly strong feelings and, yes, negative feelings—are prerequisites to intimacy. We pay a very high toll for believing that we must behave in certain patterns, fit into certain roles, and deny those feelings that come up in contradiction of those roles. When we deny our emotions we are denying a part of ourselves and contact with others. We miss discovering. We miss the unexpected. We miss a richness in life. We miss touching other people, really touching them. We miss being fully human.

When we deny that we are mad at someone or hurt by him, we are not only cutting ourselves off from our own feelings, we are putting distance between ourselves and another human being. When we are unwilling to admit and report our own insecurity, we are increasing its hold on us.

We cannot pick and choose the feelings we have. We cannot pull out only the "good" ones and share those so everyone will like us. We can't, that is, without paying the price of not being known—by ourselves or others—not being understood, not being loved. Still, we deny ourselves and hold back from showing ourselves to others, and too many of us end up lonely.

Let's examine briefly some of the fears that keep us from intimacy. I'd like to list some conditions or steps to intimacy and then note some typical fears that represent stumbling blocks.

The first and perhaps most important condition is that both parties be willing to reveal themselves to the other without the other's judgment prohibiting that. Most of us begin revealing ourselves when we are excited about meeting and being with someone new. We start telling bits and pieces of our history, our likes and dislikes, our favorite books, movies, or experiences. It's part of falling in love, of showing yourself to someone because you want to be known and in hopes he/she will love you. This begins to get sticky when the other person isn't revealing anything, when what we have to say seems negative, or when we think our feelings won't be received very well. We might say inside, "I'm afraid to let you know how I'm feeling right now; you won't like it. And you won't like me because I feel this way."

It is a very important step in a person's development when he is able to "own" his own feelings. That is, able to acknowledge them, talk about them, claim them as his own without apologizing or denying. Revealing who you are in a moment with another person not only shares part of your humanness with your partner but gives him/her a "piece of the action," so to speak. Both of you can now share in reactions and choices of what to do—if anything—about that new information.

A guideline that helps in this revelation is to view any statement from another person as a statement about that person and not about you, the listener. When you're able to do this, you can drop your defenses and hear a more valid message from the speaker about his or her feelings. Fear enters this in two ways, or from both sides of the relationship. The listener might say: "When you say you're angry, I'm always afraid I did something wrong and I freeze up." Or the speaker might say: "If I say I'm in a bad mood, I'm afraid you'll think it's your fault, so I just don't say anything." Either of these statements, unsaid, produces distance.

Another condition, or step toward intimacy, is to view differentness and disagreement as an opportunity for growth. The ways we are different from each other represent learning experiences for the person we're involved with. We're stopped when we say to ourselves: "I don't tell you things I don't like about you; I'm afraid you'd get hurt and pout or you'd get mad at me." Again, this statement of a person's likes or dislikes is a statement about that person and, if explored, can lead to some growth for both people involved.

A further step has to do with trust; it is the commitment to work through whatever feelings come up until both persons feel "clean" or cleared and settled about those feelings. This is critical. The fear that I'll reveal myself without a satisfactory response from you will often keep me quiet. The fear that we'll get into something complicated and/or painful without thoroughly working it through will keep me from raising important issues in the first place. This commitment to "stick with it" does not insure that things can always be worked out to agreement but it does say that another human being will be there to work through issues of mutual concern.

Another condition two people can agree upon is the acceptance of feelings for what they are, that they cannot be changed just because you want them to be. In my close relationships I want to accept the feelings of another without feeling like I need to change the way things are. If my partner is angry at me, I want to let him have that anger without trying to change it. Similarly, I want to own my own feelings without the pressure to change in order to make it more comfortable for my partner. This pressure to change is mostly a fear of feelings we see as negative—fear, anger, jealousy, resentment, defensiveness.

The mistake is in thinking if they are allowed their full expression they will destroy intimacy. The opposite is true.

A further step into intimacy is a clear understanding that neither person in the relationship intends to hurt the other. This may sound too simple, but if you and I can operate with this as an underlying assumption, it clears the way for us to open up, to fight, to engage each other in a way that couldn't exist if either of us were afraid of retribution or intentional pain. The fear that clogs this understanding may be that one of us will agree and the other won't or that I will hurt you unintentionally by what I reveal about myself, and you'll see it as intentional.

Finally, two people who want to move to intimacy can agree to give all they can to each other; the intent is that they will both devote time, space, and energy to each other and the relationship, that they will not hold back. It is a tragic feeling to be half of a relationship and feel like you are devoting your whole self to it while your partner seems to be interested in other things, someone else, or is too busy to give what it takes to sustain an intimate relationship. The choice and the ability to make this agreement, to give it all you're able to, is a basic requirement for two people to settle into the time and work it takes to truly be together. The fear of rejection, of being hurt, of failing, gets in the way of this: "I'm afraid to give too much to you; you won't give that much back." Or "I'm afraid to show you too much of myself; it will make me too vulnerable." Or "What would happen if I gave it all I had and still failed?"

Fear and intimacy, opposite ends of a tug of war within us. I want to express my feelings, I want to be myself, yet I am afraid to. I want to come out and meet you as a whole person and experience fully who you are, but I'm afraid to. How will you take my anger? my failures? my tenderness?

Those words, spoken or not, cry out from all of us. If we know that about each other, perhaps we can take a step closer together, not denying that we are afraid, but taking our fear with us.

CHAPTER 7

Fear in the world

Many of the social directions we have taken in the past fifty years make up a good recipe for fear. Rapid change, new environments, crowded conditions, more and more noise, an overload of stimuli—things that we are inherently afraid of or that encourage fear.

We have changed ourselves, our view of ourselves, and the world around us; we have abandoned ways and institutions our parents and grandparents revered; we move more often; we travel at a faster pace; we have crammed ourselves closer and closer together in dirty, traffic-clogged cities and we are abandoning groups—marriages, families, neighborhoods, and small towns—that brought us a certain security and intimacy.

This age also seems a time when we are discovering how much we don't know, about ourselves and the universe in which we live. Our solar system seems more real to us than ever, yet, in a broader perspective, we are just beginning to find out about it. Beyond, in thousands of other galaxies and swirling around other stars and suns, wait even more questions for us to answer and space for us to explore.

Another frontier calls within the boundaries of every human body. Most of us do not experience the full range of our emotions or know the power of our brain or our will. Somewhere, in a space and time frame we don't know much about, the supernatural calls to some of us; events and forces we can't explain wait for our exploration.

In short, it is an easy time to be afraid, just as it is a time for excitement and challenge. There seems to be more we can't predict; events we can't influence; conditions we can't control. There is a greater awareness of the crime and threats we inflict on one another, individual and nation, just as we are more aware of our alienation and loneliness.

Fear plays a major role in this modern scenario. It not only affects our intimate, one-to-one relationships, but our families, our neighborhoods, our cities, our social decisions, our politics. The way we live together is governed by fear far more than we realize.

We have seen how fear affects us as individual animals—we tighten up, speed up our systems inside, prepare for concealment, flight, and defense, if necessary. Our body is ready to defend, when frightened; it is not ready to reason, to make decisions, or to extend itself to another. We will choose escape, even into pain, instead of facing a fear. And, as our avoidance of our fear goes on, we adopt a casual, almost routine way to escape or hide ourselves; our fear-induced behavior seems "normal."

Collectively, fear affects us in similar ways. We will band together with others of a like appearance and/or conviction. We will shore up defenses that will preserve our group and its norms of behavior. The more afraid we become, the more forceful will be our rejection of outsiders; we will make ready for battle if necessary. Reason does not appeal to us at these threatening times; we are too afraid and defensive against change. We will choose the pain of alienation, financial hardship, fighting in the streets, warping ourselves, and our children instead of dealing openly with what we are afraid of.

One of the most visual examples of our individual fear manifesting itself socially takes place in interactions between the races. A recent example is what took place in Boston in 1974 when that city was undergoing the strains of forced integration in its schools. There, after ten years of flirting and playing possum with school integration and twenty years after the Supreme Court decided our schools should be black and white together, Boston exploded with demonstrations, boycotts, and violence, when South Boston schools were integrated.

The October 14 *Washington Post* carried a story that outlined the situation and the feelings behind it:

> Fear is the common denominator here, fear that all of the institutions the working man has relied upon so strongly—the church, the city hall, the police—have finally turned against him.
>
> The whole thing is crazy, unbelievable. You know who the new American nigger is? It's the "working man," said a white man in South Boston as he watched a phalanx of riot equipped police move down his street.
>
> That fear and its accompanying resentment and anger exploded—predictably, according to some—in the past four weeks into ugly mob violence reminiscent of Little Rock, Selma, and the other battlegrounds of desegregation in the South in the 1950s and 1960s.[1]

The story points out that the two communities that are most in conflict with each other, white South Boston and black Roxbury, are amazingly alike, except for the color of the residents' skin. The economic base for the two communities are blue-collar workers; the percentage of professional or technical workers in white South Boston is 12.4 percent versus 17 percent in black Roxbury; the percentage of domestics employed is 18 percent in the white community and 22.2 percent in the black community; the average income is $6,588 in Roxbury and though it is $2,000 higher in South Boston there are more unemployed in Roxbury, lowering the average figure. Both are lower than the Boston average.

In both communities there was acknowledged proudly a sense of kinship and community, a feeling that individuals know

---

[1] *Washington Post*, October 14, 1974, Sec. A, p. 1.

their neighbors and could count on them in an emergency. There was another mutual feeling reported. Residents of South Boston were afraid to send their children into Roxbury and black parents were afraid to send their children into South Boston.

Robert Schwartz, an adviser to Boston mayor Kevin White, pointed to a source of the conflict in the same article:

> How can you maintain this strong neighborhood attachment and at the same time get people to realize that those neighborhoods are enclaves, fortresses in effect, and that kids have to cross the boundaries sooner or later, both coming in and going out?
>
> But there is an absolute hostility to outsiders, and when it comes to blacks, hostility is an understatement. It is a fear of other neighborhoods; it is a fear that says if a kid goes out and mixes with other kids, that is going to lead to the destruction of the neighborhood.

Schwartz puts his finger on two of our most common fears—the fear of "outsiders" and the fear that our community, both physical and emotional, will break down. Blacks, or any persons of a different skin color, are easily identifiable "outsiders." Without any further knowledge of who a black person is or any reasoning of how much he is like a white person, he is easily labeled, put into a box and defended against.

In situations like the one in South Boston, individual feelings run high and find even more strength in expression with others in like groups. Whites and blacks are afraid of each other. They each resent the taking away of their freedom of choice (as they see it). They are angry at being forced into a public policy they do not agree with. They are afraid their children will be hurt. They feel confused, fed up, frustrated and, on top of all of that, impotent to do anything to change the situation. These are feelings that are common in America today.

Where was the force, in this case, to help Boston heal itself? Where was the agency, publication, institution, or the individual who would help a community prepare itself for the change that was coming and to help resolve feelings that would surely rise?

Boston had ten years to face the problem of school integration, since the state first passed its racial imbalance law in

1965. Public officials, private businessmen, the newspapers and television stations, all could have learned lessons from southern states. Yet, in one of the most enlightened and liberal of all the states, we have had a repetition of the bitterness, fear, and anger we have seen for years expressed in the withdrawal of children from school and physical violence. Flee. Hide. Defend. Fight.

It is natural that these basic emotions—fear, anger, frustration, and the sense of powerlessness—find their way into our political choices. Further, the fear we have is not only reflected in our political choices, but it influences our political leaders in forming national and international policies. Fear affects our politics profoundly and every politician—and those who market them—know it.

Psychologist Rollo May has a theory that voters, faced with unsettling times and rapid social change, will retreat, out of fear, into apathy. He maintains they did just that in 1972 when they elected Richard Nixon in a landslide but "undervoted" election.

We can paint a picture of the American voter in the fall of that year—threatened by rising welfare costs, afraid of integration (particularly by busing), still tangled up with a devisive war in Vietnam, astonished by a rising crime rate, and faced with an upward spiral of prices. To vote for Democrat George McGovern would have been to vote for even more change—election reform, welfare law reform, a flat-out withdrawal from Vietnam, plus controversial stands on homosexuality and abortion.

Richard Nixon did not conduct an active, issue-oriented campaign. He had a stable of surrogate campaigners who toured the country on his behalf while McGovern was forced to reach farther and farther for issues that would touch the voters and persuade them to change their mind.

An unconscious—or very conscious—reaction of a voter might have been: "I am weary and frightened by all that's going on around me. I do not want more change; I want less. I want to keep some things around me I can depend on. I don't want to rock the boat anymore."

Another reaction, looking at the extremely low percentage of voters that turned out, might have been one of helplessness and impotency. Faced with a hit and miss campaign where one of the candidates seemed to be missing, and harboring the feeling that their vote didn't matter, voters stayed away from the polls in record numbers.

We know that helplessness or the feeling that a person can't affect the situation he's in only increases his fear and contributes to his dis-ease. That powerlessness—the feeling that we cannot direct our own lives and maintain a strong sense of individual worth—is extremely important in a democratic society. The more helpless we are, the more afraid we are. The more afraid we are, the more we retreat into emotional and physical shells, protecting our ego, our body, and our private property. The less we move out into any sense of community with our neighbors, be they across the street or across the country, the less we exercise our right to express ourselves and take the power and responsibility that each individual needs and the society needs to deal with the complex problems that face us.

In a real sense, whatever campaign threats or promises we make that contribute to an individual's sense of powerlessness or fear puts another nail in the coffin of our democratic process.

Beyond the matter of choosing political leaders is the influence of fear on these leaders once they are in office. There has been a limited amount of research on the role emotions and sexual and racial stereotypes play in the formation of national and international policies, but if we look closely at the media and some popular books, examples present themselves.

The fear of outsiders, for instance, is no special purview of whites in South Boston, or of whites period. It reaches into all races and classes, even, in the view of some, into the highest elected office in America.

Consider these views, by Washington-based writer Peter Rand and two people he interviewed about Gerald Ford:

> He [Ford] has kept the ghetto happy back home, and it's doubtful you'll hear the Urban League making big noises about Ford. Most significantly though, Ford has represented the fear of his community before the nation.
>
> "I don't think he'd recognize it as such," says the Rev. Duncan Littlefair of Grand Rapids, "but he's scared and they're all scared here."
>
> Rev. Littlefair is the rector of the Fountain Street Church, once a Baptist church, now simply referred to as "the liberal

church." Rev. Littlefair is a vigorous, blue-eyed Michigander in his sixties who has struggled for years against Grand Rapids' obstinacy to change. "Ford isn't a bad man, but he's dumb, dumb," he says. . . . "He shouldn't be dumb, either. He went to school just like everybody else. Michigan, Yale. But you see, he lacks depth. He has a righteousness that gets him into that fringe stuff, like the Douglas impeachment thing. It's just fear."

Fear of what? Jean McKee, who once said you could only defeat Ford in a local election if you caught him raping a nun, maintains that it's the simple fear of outsiders. "It's like this here," she says, making a circle with her thumbs and forefingers. "He's inside with his community, and he can't relate to the people outside it. He can barely perceive that they have needs that may differ from the mainstream in these parts."

The fear that characterizes Grand Rapids to the liberals who live there is projected onto the nation by Gerald Ford when he votes for greater defense spending, when he says, as he did in 1965, "If we give up in South Vietnam, it would give up Southeast Asia . . . and our defense lines would be driven back to the Hawaiian Islands."

"Ford is adamant about the military," Rev. Littlefair says. "It's one thing he isn't rational about at all. More spending, more guns, keep the Communists out—why he's even against détente now."

Without regard to Rand's or the Rev. Littlefair's political views about Ford, they underline important points about fear in our domestic and international politics. Politicians are human beings, including the President; we often forget that. They are raised by other imperfect human beings and grow up with many of the same fears we all have. Fear of strangers and outsiders is one; fear of rejection another. Fear that their image of themselves may be threatened is still another.

In the film *Hearts and Minds*, filmmaker Peter Davies examined some of the American values that led to our involvement in Vietnam and our dogged continuation of that frustrating and tragic war. One of the things he focused on was the attitude of masculine toughness, or "macho," as reflected in football, the all-American game. He pictured, in a high school football coach and the fans and in Presidents and presidential advisers, the desire to win at all costs, the hyping up of players to preserve their masculine image by dominating others and the disgrace of losing face by losing the game.

The desire to dominate, to win at all costs, leads to violence, in marriages as well as in international relationships. It became clear in the Pentagon Papers, when they were made public, how this "macho" attitude had influenced our policy in Vietnam. A memo from an assistant to then Secretary of Defense Robert McNamara in 1965 outlined the U.S. aims in continuing the conflict. According to that memo, our aims in Southeast Asia were: "70 percent, to avoid a humiliating United States defeat . . . 20 percent, to keep South Vietnam . . . from Chinese hands . . . 10 percent, to permit the people of South Vietnam to enjoy a better freer way of life." How do these goals fit in with our announced policy? What kind of connections can you make between a national policy "to avoid humiliation" and personal feelings of individuals in the Department of Defense and the executive branch that have to do with the fear of failure and the need to dominate?

It is tragic to think of the energy, the spirit, and the human lives that were wasted in Vietnam. It is even more discouraging and disheartening to think that even part of it sprang from such unfortunate roots.

Another hint at how fear seeps into vital world issues, this from a UPI story in the spring of 1975:

> Former deputy Secretary of Defense Paul Nitze charged Friday that former President Richard Nixon's refusal to permit the use of American interpreters hampered U.S. negotiations at the first strategic arms limitation talks.
>
> He said, in a TV interview on ABC's "AM America," that Mr. Nixon took this stand because he had an obsession with secrecy—even secrecy within his own government.
>
> "He wasn't confident that all those working in the executive branch were totally loyal and considered secure from his standpoint. He was afraid that people not really wholly within his confidence might talk to others within the U.S. executive branch," Nitze said.
>
> Nitze went on to say that this fear of Nixon's complicated the SALT talks: ". . . the result was that we who were negotiating at the lower levels were never quite sure what had transpired at the higher level."

Here is an example of one man's fear and insecurity affecting negotiations for the limitations of atomic weapons, getting in the way of talks dealing with whether or not we're going to blow each other up.

The fears of Richard Nixon and Gerald Ford are but reflections of fears we all experience. These same kinds of fears influence all of us at one level or another in how we make decisions, how we manage conflict, how we react to crisis. And even though our fears go unattended, they govern us. Politicians do not escape, any more than you or I.

When we perceive a threat by outsiders, we bristle and defend. We are afraid and we fight—as we did in Boston and as we have in Little Rock and Vietnam. We are afraid and we vote for money to defend ourselves or we vote for a policy that will preserve what we have and keep someone else from getting it. The stronger we perceive the threat, the more hostile our reaction. Individuals and nations share this tendency.

What we lack is any kind of broad-based effort to help us understand ourselves and the way we interact. We have marriage counselors and business consultants to resolve contract disputes. Labor negotiators heal wounds between workers and management. Why can't we have an agency to help neighborhoods and communities understand each other, to help us meet each other's needs, to prepare us for change, and to deal with the fact that emotions underlie so much of our public behavior? Instead we go on dealing with eruptions, crises, boils on the skin of the body politic, trying to suppress and control violence instead of dealing with its causes.

Nowhere is this more evident than in the news media that serve our communities. Television news programs and newspapers thrive on conflict, violence, and "public eruptions." We are bombarded with a daily dose of murder, rape, robbery, political scandal, and accidental mayhem. We are spoon-fed instances of man's inhumanity.

I'd like to examine the media briefly with regard to the role they play in increasing or decreasing our fear. I want to look at the media and measure them against a question that is at the root of communication: What is the information we are conveying to one another doing to bring us together?

The vast and powerful news media we have set up to communicate have a day-by-day opportunity—and challenge—to give us information that can help us with psychic and physical survival. They can give us valuable information about things and people from whom we are alienated, as well as prepare us for social change. They can help decrease our fears and give us a sense of potency as individual citizens.

Instead, in the vast majority of our news reports we are given what amounts to a rhythmic hammering of danger signals. These cues—three women were raped in the park last night, violence broke out at an elementary school on the first day of mandatory busing, four children and two adults died in a head-on crash on Highway 29—are factual. But, for the most part, they go unexplained. They lack context, background, and perspective and they are far from balanced with information that lies beneath the surface event.

Try a little test for yourself. Read through a daily newspaper or monitor an evening newscast to try and determine what we as a society are saying to each other. Remember, the various news media are only a part, but a big part, of the way we as a community of people are talking to one another.

Divide the stories into categories: stories that in some way meet a need you have, help you understand yourself or someone else in your community, give you some new information or perspective on how you can improve the quality of your life or your effectiveness as a citizen. A second category would be stories and/or pictures that make you feel defensive, alienated, helpless, frustrated, or fearful of what is going to happen. I suspect you will have to open a crack in a pretty thick layer that normally protects us from much of the news and, I warn you, the result of this kind of test can be depressing.

How often do you see stories about every particular involved in a rape—the who, where, when, why and how? How is rape related to our society's attitude about sex? What laws, if any, do we need to change, to attack the underlying reasons for rape? What can you, as an individual, do, besides arm yourself, to help in your neighborhood? What are police doing? What is city hall doing? What is the newspaper doing?

The information we most often get is in the form of repeated cues that tap into our fear, just as the white side of the box panicked the white rats about to be shocked and just as the dimming lights frightened the dogs in the experiments we read about in Chapter 2. We are given the danger signal and we react out of our fear.

One small example. In the fall of 1974, we were overwhelmed with the news and the actuality of rising prices. One of the most obvious products affected was sugar. Sugar prices tripled in one year and we were regularly presented the news that the price of raw sugar had gone up, that supermarkets were rationing the amounts customers could buy, that hoarding was going on in many cities, and that things were bound to get worse. Bad news. What were we going to do when we couldn't afford sugar any more? What was causing the high prices? What could we do about it? These questions weren't answered. We were getting plenty of information to alarm us; remember, this is just one product that most of us use every day in our homes and inflation affected all of them. But where was the "news" that would help us deal with this problem?

One evening Walter Cronkite just about knocked me off my chair. After a typical filmed report that showed checkers stamping new high prices on bags of sugar and making signs that said "limit, one bag per customer," Walter came back on the air and said words to this effect: We don't really need sugar anyway. It is a luxury in American diets. Doctors tell us that it is very high in calories and the carbohydrates we get from it can easily be obtained from carrots, beans, and other vegetables.

Here was something that made us feel a little bit better. Here was a crack in the door and we could see some light. Here was maybe 10 seconds on the air that told us: "It's OK, maybe this will work out for the better anyway. You may have to change your eating habits a bit, but you may be better off." Cronkite could have gone on to say that we use more sugar than any other nation, that it's a terrible food nutritionally and if we stopped using it we would appreciate to a much greater degree the natural sweet taste in the other foods we eat. But it was a start.

That kind of information is readily available, to Cronkite and to you and me, but it does not fit the definition of what the great majority of journalists in this country considers "news"; hence it does not find its way into our homes via the media we have come to depend on.

In the FBI building in Washington there used to be a display that informed touring visitors about the agency's war on crime. Part of the display was a red light that, based on an average frequency, blinked every time a crime was committed somewhere in the country. Can you imagine having a light like that in your house? How would you begin to feel after a while? Afraid? Defensive? Protective?

It seems to me that we have the equivalent of that red light; we turn it on in the evening to get the news and we pick it up on our doorstep. Each gives us our daily dose of what there is in the world to be afraid of.

This hammering away at our fear and helplessness is by no means limited to the news staffs of television or the newspapers. The "entertainment" programming on television and the motion picture industry has an effect too. A quick survey of the television programming in a major market will reveal that there are three to five programs every night of the year, not counting motion pictures, that reel off episodes of crime and violence. As children and as adults, we are constantly reminded of how violent the world is and how tough, how thick-skinned we must be to cope. We see countless ways in which we can die. Rare is the program that reveals the true nature of police work, or puts crime in any kind of perspective, or helps us understand our role in dealing with crime, or reveals what really happens to persons outside the law when they contact our criminal justice system.

These kinds of messages are not dramatized as easily; it takes a modicum of imagination to turn them into saleable scripts. But it can be done; this small example comes to mind. One episode of "The Streets of San Francisco," an hour-long show about police work in that California city, dealt with child abuse. In the beginning of the show there was a scene in which a thirteen-year-old boy was hit by his stepfather, and when police were called to check it out, they discovered his body was covered with scars and welts.

Now this sets us up. The usual show, with some twists and turns and false leads to keep us interested, will lead to the apprehension of the guilty party and the kid will find some relief. We are left with little understanding of the larger picture of child abuse. In this segment, however, there was something added, five minutes that made the hour almost worthwhile. In the course of their investigation, the inspectors go into a center that helps parents and others deal with child abuse. During a brief talk with the man who ran the center, himself a father who used to beat his child, we learn how many children are abused each year, what some of the causes are, that people can be reformed, and where to turn for help. It was obvious; still, it worked, and it took this segment out of the usual cops-and-robbers, good-guy–bad-guy doldrums for at least one scene.

That is just one small example of what could be done in television programming, in the context of entertainment, to help us better understand one another and the communities in which we live. It is information that increases our potency as individuals and helps us deal with an increasingly complex and frightening world.

The media is especially important to me; I have worked in it and understand it more than I do the other systems that serve our society. From a broad perspective, the free enterprise system made up of newspapers, magazines, and television is the source I look to for connection with other human beings. They can systematically feed me information that tends to make me afraid of my neighbors, across the street and across the globe, or they can provide me with information that helps me understand and celebrate my commonality with and my differences from other people.

We are in the global electronic village McLuhan has talked about. We have the technology that can provide us with empathy and understanding for a man in Kenya, a woman in Canton, or a child in Argentina. It won't do that if we continue to use our communications channels solely for news of crisis, violence, and disaster.

Most of us will have little first-hand experience with real "outsiders." Although we are probably the most mobile country on earth in a very mobile age, most people deal with the same people in their work and social lives and depend on that regularity and sameness for much of their security. This, of course, has gone on for centuries, but now, more than ever, we can see how the rest of the world exists in living color. And others can see how we live. We can see that there is a great deal to be afraid of "out there,"—famine, war, disease, revolution. Now it all seems suddenly closer to us, more real, more connected. We realize that we *are* all in this together and we have a very critical choice—to react out of our fear or out of our love. We can defend, conceal ourselves, and flee from one another or we can be open, sharing, and move toward one another. The information we get, through our media, plays a critical role in that choice.

Our collective media—certainly including the pervasive advertising industry—play into another combination of fear and power and responsibility. It is a combination that affects our social, political, and religious institutions as well as our one-to-one relationships.

We deify things—people, animals, institutions, groups, and imaginary beings. People have deified things for a long time and we are no different in that respect. Myths, traditions, folklore, and rituals historically surround gods in primitive cultures; so it is with ours. Three important things happen when, either as a people or as individuals, we boost someone or something to that position: they are distanced from us, we vest an inordinate amount of power in them, and we begin to fear them. The greater the mystery that surrounds the person or institution we deify, the greater our fear is, the more power we lose, and the less responsibility we take for ourselves.

Try to come up with a list of the things you think you—and we as a society—may have deified. That we respect or worship them, in the terms we usually think of, is not necessarily a guideline. Think about things that we surround with mystery, money, power, and a certain aura of fear.

I think about the FBI, movie stars, rock stars, animals such as sharks, wolves, and killer whales, money, the police, death, the Kennedys, AT&T, athletes (superstars), banks, sex, lawyers, and journalists. We deified Richard Nixon and when we found out his feet were made of clay too, we stripped him of the power, reverence, and fear that we had given him.

Let's take an example from which most of us are removed but which illustrates the point well. Think of the myths, as well as the aura of fear, that grew up around the wolf. We didn't know much about the wolf, but we thought of it as a vicious man-eating predator, capable of great feats of strength and endurance. Tales of horror came out of Canada and northern United States about the bloodthirsty wolf. Only recently, with information from people who have seen wolves' lives first-hand for an extended period of time, have we learned the truth. Wolves are remarkable animals but not at all like what we had believed. To the degree that any of us were afraid of wolves, we gave up an unnecessary amount of power to them. Not that we shouldn't show caution and treat them with a healthy respect, but in a posture of inordinate fear we rob ourselves of our own abilities and effectiveness.

The same general things hold true about our relationships with other people and with institutions. When we assign them more power than they deserve, we give away our own. It is not so much that we are afraid of them, in the way we usually think of it, but that we are afraid to be ourselves with them.

This is important in a marriage or in a relationship with a government institution. A woman, for instance, who has put her husband on a pedestal, who tries to meet his every need and leaves the major decisions about the course of their lives up to him, has, to a degree, deified him. She has given up her power to her husband and this is invariably accompanied by feelings of fear and impotency on her part. In fact, the deification of her husband in the first place may have sprung from the fear of taking responsibility for herself and running her own life.

We behave in much the same way with government agencies and big business. We have handed them an extraordinary amount of power over our lives. Though it might be stretching it to say that many Americans are afraid of the phone company, for instance, I think many of us are afraid of what this and other similar agencies can do to us. They can ruin our credit rating, cut off one of our means of communication (or our power or water or other services), contact our employers and attach our salaries, or bring us to court to face a battery of lawyers. They are formidable enemies, if crossed.

Sometimes it seems as if the individual is faced with a network of institutions that have grown too big and too formidable for him to deal with or affect. We have elected people to serve us in local, state, and federal governments. We have formed agencies to meet our vital needs in our communities. Now we seem faced with the reality that these bodies are complex and unresponsive; that they dominate our lives in ways we don't want. We have given up too much of our individual power and handed it over to courts, agencies, commissions, departments, councils, and assemblies; we have given up our own responsibility. We have spun our own web of helplessness, fear, and apathy. Faced more and more with the prospect that we can't affect our own lives, we retreat into our plaster casts of conformity and desensitized existence.

Occasionally we see an example of a person who successfully fights "the system" and it is relatively big news. Sometimes we may experience first-hand that some of the feelings we have, of fear, helplessness, and apathy, are unfounded. We can take steps toward making our own decisions in a close relationship and see that maybe we have created a monster that wasn't there. We can unlearn the fear, for instance that an outsider always needs to be feared and defended against. We can find out how much of a friend a stranger of another race or culture can be if we overcome the fear we have.

We can begin to take on the feeling that we as individuals are more important than we have believed, that we are the ones being served by the institutions and agencies we have built, not the other way around. We can begin to experience our own power and responsibility and move out of the quicksand of fear and apathy.

The important step seems the first one, the first courageous step we take in our own personal life to move through our fear and take the power we have given up to others. How does this then affect us in our community and in our society?

Alan Paton of South Africa explores the point with regard to race relations in his own country:

> . . . in spite of all this one goes on believing in a nonracial unity that can transcend racial difference. This is something that one has come to believe through experience of personal relationships, and it may be that what is possible in personal relationships

is not possible in society. There have been many examples in history where two individuals from mutually hostile groups have greatly loved one another.

Now, is it possible or is it not possible to realize in society what one has realized in personal relationships? I believe one cannot answer the question. All that one can say is that there is within one an impulse to try to realize it, that this impulse is an integral part of one's self and that it must be obeyed, for to disobey it is to do damage to the integrity of one's self. And what is more, one has fortunately already learned the lesson that a failure, or a measure of failure, to realize some social or political aim can be compensated for to a tremendous degree by the depth and warmth of one's personal relationships.[2]

The question fascinates me: Can we realize in society what we have learned and done in our personal relationships? That is, can I take the learnings I have about my own fear and apply them to my neighborhood, my city? Can I hope for and work for a public policy that reflects a humanitarian lesson I have learned myself, a struggle I have overcome?

My answer has to be yes, though I think it is a question that each person has to answer for himself. It is a delicate task and one that takes a great deal of courage and determination. Yet I believe this is a source of creative social change. One man's lesson in facing his fear, for instance, can be learned by his family, his neighbors, his city, and even his country, if his message is strong enough and there are people willing to listen.

I have a basic belief that is at the heart of this: each of us must take responsibility for nurturing the creative, expressive, powerful parts of ourselves if we are to form and re-form the social systems that serve us and build the kind of human communities we want to live in. We can no longer leave this task solely up to a representative or an institution; we cannot demand or expect responsiveness, openness, trust, or creativity from others in our lives if *we* do not have those qualities too.

For each of us to acknowledge and express our full, lively personhood to one another is the beginning of community, that mysterious and wonderful union of two or more human beings.

[2] Alan Paton, "The Challenge of Fear," *Saturday Review*, September 9, 1967, p. 21.

When we begin to leave that openness, trust, and expressions of who we are behind us, the breakdown of community begins. I believe that is the essential nature of crime, violence, and apathy—the breakdown of community. We commit crimes against one another because, ultimately, we don't care for one another. We commit crimes against ourselves because we don't love ourselves. Crimes include robbery, rape, and murder, but also callousness, lack of respect, indifference, arrogance, and manipulation.

We commit these personal crimes on one another every day and from these day-by-day roots our social ills grow. The easiest way for me to talk about a way out of this is to explore some concepts of creativity. There are some among us—creative politicians, spiritual leaders, artists, educators, writers, and others—who take some measure of the message going on inside them and make a personal statement to a larger audience. But this choice is open to many more of us than respond to it. This willingness to remain open, to express your truth, to respond to human needs, and make commitments is possible for each of us. It is not easy, but it is worth it. It is a struggle against the pressure to conform and against fear.

This battle of fear and creativity is vitally important to each one of us, not just the people who choose to follow their strong personal instincts, but to each of us as members of the human community.

Just who are these magical creative people I'm talking about and how do they live their lives?

The kind of people I'm talking about have certain things in common: they are willing to express themselves; they use their imagination; they exercise personal taste; they are unique and know it; they will evaluate themselves and make their own judgments; they are willing to be different from the norm; they are willing to try something new.

How is that different from what you are willing to do?

We can all express ourselves, in one way or another—with our mouths, with our hands, our bodies; in the kitchen, in the bedroom, in the sewing room, the laboratory, the classroom. We all have imagination, the formation of images in our heads which, as yet, do not exist in reality. What we often lack is the courage to acknowledge and/or express those imaginings.

We all have taste. We grow up with preferences, likes and dislikes, that we express daily in the way we live our lives and choose the things with which we surround ourselves. What we often lack is the courage to take responsibility for our own taste, to thoroughly respond to our own wants and make choices about our environment.

We are unique, from our fingerprints to our voices, from the moment and circumstances of our birth, to the way we're doing whatever it is we're doing at the moment. When we deny our individuality and accept the trappings of conformity, it is more out of a lack of awareness and fear than anything else.

Most creative people have what is called "an internal locus of evaluation"; that is, their word about what is good and bad for them is more important than someone else's. Their opinion of their own work and their own way of life governs them more than their father's word, their mate's opinion, or the reactions of critics—real or imagined. It is, of course, easier to let other people decide.

The willingness to be different follows closely behind. We *are* different from one another, but to *be* different—that's not easy. Being yourself is the hardest thing there is in life, e. e. cummings believes, because the world is full of people who will tell you who you are and what you should be doing. And you are full of ghosts of the past and fears of your future who may not approve of who you are. It is difficult. You have to keep doing it over and over, being yourself.

To try the new, to experiment, to combine things that haven't gone together before, to juggle elements of a problem, experiment, or relationship—that's one of the most crucial elements of being creative. The courage to move into the unknown is what has moved mankind, individually and collectively, ahead since there was a mankind to talk about. Each of us has our own personal frontier; to the degree that we move into that unknown is the degree we will grow.

The theme that runs through most of this for me is *the willingness to be known,* in various modes and expressions; the courage to be and share your full self. It sounds abstract and easy, but it is a specific quality and it is very hard to achieve.

We have some tough choices ahead as social beings. Governments may consider it more necessary than ever to control personal freedom in order to meet crises in population control, food supplies, environmental controls, and social unrest. But against that backdrop we are called to a society where individual choice, individual expression, and humanistic values would govern our political acts.

How we respond, as individuals, to that choice is critical. I believe your own struggle, with your emerging person and with your fear, is at the heart of it. Each of us is moved by our own inner images, songs, and rhythms. The externalization of this is at the core of the creative process. There are many things that stand in our way: constant change, an overload of stimuli, our own laziness, drugs, the fear of rejection, the judgment of others, the fear of failure—a thousand ways to be discouraged, a thousand forces that will help you retreat into your shell. If each of us can summon up the courage to be more of our unique self, to express who we are, to seize our own personal power, individuals and governments will have little choice but to respond to us as we are.

I hope I have made it clear how important a cornerstone fear is in all of this. The fear of change, the fear of rejection, the fear of failure, the fear of loss of control—all drain us of our power, as individuals and as nations. When this fear becomes too strong, what political or social power a man has will become warped; he will abrogate the rights of others; he will make changes designed only to hold onto what power he has left; he will deny rules and laws and claim that he is saving them. To preserve human values, he may use methods incompatible with our deepest and best human feelings. And, of course, he will not admit he is afraid.

Subjected to this kind of control, others may wither and retreat. Stunned and alarmed, overwhelmed and afraid, they might easily retreat into a shell in which their senses are dulled and their own views of who they are become stifled. That very process of retreat is what breaks down intimacy, community, and cooperation—among individuals and among nations.

You do have a choice in all this. There is no getting away from it, in fact. To do nothing is a choice. To retreat, out of fear or apathy, is to give up power to someone else. To move out, to express, to share, to become known all involve another choice, counterbalancing your fears. The choice each of us makes has very much to do with the kind of neighborhood, city, and global community we hope to build.

PART THREE

*New
Perspectives*

CHAPTER 8

Fear and desire

> *One is never taken care of; that life is a naked battle between fear and desire, and that fear is kept in abeyance only through the recurrent surge of desire; that desire is whetted only if it is reinforced by the capacity to experience oneself; that the capacity to experience oneself is everything.*[1]
>
> VIVIAN GORNICK

In this chapter, I want to play with the themes of fear and desire and experiencing oneself, to pit them against one another and have you try the same, for yourself, in your own way. If they fit, good; if not, perhaps we can learn from that.

I have experienced far too many people—for moments and for years—who do not want badly enough what they want. I know a woman who wants an intimate relationship with a man, but will do nothing about it; I know a man who wants a job in journalism, but sits transfixed by his own fear and indecision, doing nothing but taking occasional part-time jobs; I know another man who wants to quit the job he's in and pursue his own interests for a while, but he goes back, day after day, fearful that he'll lose his status, his income, and his daily structure if he

---

[1] From Vivian Gornick, "Toward a Definition of the Female Sensibility," *The Village Voice*, May 31, 1973. Reprinted by permission of The Village Voice. Copyright © The Village Voice, Inc., 1973.

quits. Each of us probably knows someone who says he or she wants something but does nothing about it.

This leads to the first idea I want to explore: What I want most is what I am most afraid of. And the twist: What I am most afraid of is what I want most. Imagine something that you are afraid of—a person, a situation, a condition. What is it in that you want? What is it that you are drawn to yet defensive against? What is the strange mix of fear and desire that attracts and repels you?

Let's try an example. I'm a housewife; I've been raising children and keeping house for my family for fifteen years. What I want now is to get out of the house, to pursue some interests that have nothing to do with my husband or children. I'd like to get a part-time job and take a class in painting. Fantasies of what this would be like keep floating through my mind—some independence, some time to myself, exposure to new people, a chance to express myself in art. I am drawn to this unmistakably, not just as a lark or something to take up time, but I *want* this for myself.

At the same time, I'm very afraid of it. It means changing things, changing the routine of the house, changing my relationship with my husband and my children. It may mean shedding some old roles and making me a little less important to the family than I have been. Maybe they won't need me as much. And the things I say I want—maybe I don't have the skills to get a job, any job. Maybe it would be a drag and more trouble than it's worth; it might take more time than I want to give and more money than it returns. Painting—maybe I've lost whatever touch I had; what if my husband laughs at me; or the instructor does? Fear after fear flows through the floodgate when I start to realize what I really want and how much I want it.

Let's try another example. I am a lonely man, divorced now for two years and not in any kind of close relationship with a woman. I want that very much; let's be specific, I want to become closer to Barbara. I've known her now for a year, on a kind of superficial level, and feel very attracted to her. I'd like to spend more time with her, and I'm sexually attracted to her. Yet, I've not asked her to spend time with me and when I'm with her I feel awkward and hesitant—I'm afraid. I don't know how she feels about me. Maybe she doesn't like the way I look. If I ask her I might get turned down; I don't need that rejection right now. Besides, if we did spend time together it probably wouldn't last; I have a way of getting out of these things before too long. Fear on top of fear holds me down in a quicksand of inactivity. I want it. I am afraid of it. As long as my fear is stronger than my want, I will remain here, defended, looking out at the world.

It seems as if our fear grows as does our desire. It would be too easy if, when we wanted something very much, our level of fear were much lower than our desire. But the level of our fear, like some knowing percolator, bubbles right up to the top to meet head-on the things we want the most.

And is it true that the things we are most afraid of we really somehow want? Do we harbor somewhere in our unconscious self a strong yearning for the very things we profess the most fear for?

I have felt this way about loss of control. A group leader and counselor I came across in the East says that most of us go through our lives as if we were half-crazed and full of pent-up passions we are scared to death to let out. We would be put away—and even not loved by our friends—if we let out the emotion that we have inside.

I am afraid to lose control. I am afraid I will hurt someone, say some things I don't really mean, that I will care for someone too much or make a fool of myself. But, God, how I want to. Wouldn't it be a lovely feeling to let it all go. To hell with what people think. I really want to say how angry I am. I want to get rid of some of this closed-up anger and tension. I want to dance in the street. I want to hug you and fondle you, right here in front of everyone.

My fear comes first, but lurking underneath is the unexpressed desire to break out, to be my crazy, unbridled self.

Another example: I am afraid to show people what I write. I write some poetry and write in my journal regularly, but I'm afraid to show it to anyone else. They wouldn't understand it. They might even laugh at it. Besides, it is too personal. On the other hand, I'd really like to show it to someone else and have that person understand some of the things that are important to me. I'd like to use some of the things I've written to make contact with someone else who might feel the same way. He (or she) could find out some things about me, some things that are hard to reveal, but are very important parts of me. Yes, I want to do that.

The see-saw struggle goes on. The two sides of our nature wrestle with each other, back and forth—fear and desire, desire and fear. If we're lucky, we're aware of it and can sense the nature of the conflict within us. We can weigh our wants and our fears; we can examine and explore them and choose what our responses will be. The battle goes on, wringing our bodies and muddling our heads with tension.

As one writer from a California growth center puts it:

> However complex we are as human beings, there is an overriding logic to our responses: we are motivated by our needs and deterred by our fear. Thus, the search must be directed inward, for here lies the key to change, to inner harmony and fulfillment.
>
> If we would fulfill our needs, we must objectively recognize our needs: emotional, intellectual, physical, and spiritual. If we would seek inner harmony, we necessarily need to know the source of our inner conflicts. If we would realize our full capabilities, we benefit by first discovering the invisible chains which hold us back.

To have values is part of our uniqueness as individuals and human beings. To want is inescapable. To go after what you want is risky; you expose yourself as human, vulnerable. Failure and rejection, however you interpret them, await you. Fear will always accompany what you want badly.

To consistently yield to fear is to have what you want continually denied. To make no moves, to take half-hearted action, is to deny yourself. What this battle of fear and desire becomes in the end is a dance of constricting, incapacitating, stagnating fears and expanding, creative, joy-giving satisfaction. Self-affirmation or self-denial. Death or life.

Perhaps in each of these examples we are talking about fears could easily be identified in other ways—fear of failure, rejection, being vulnerable, or losing love. But it helps for me to put on new glasses sometimes, new ways of looking at the world to see what I can learn. To take some measure of what I am

afraid of and to see what I want and realize how afraid of it I a_
helps me. It gives me a bigger handle on the world. It points out
directions I can move in, when and if I want to.

I think what this theory says, in a more accurate way, is
that something you want is always *accompanied* by fear. Perhaps
we are not always afraid of the person, working situation, place,
or emotional state that we want to get to, but that we won't get
it; or will. One further example might make this more clear.

I have a lot of fantasies about living in the country; many of
us do, I think. I dream about leaving the rush and crush of the
city and suburbs and moving to a house off in the woods. I could
write in peace and quiet, have more space, more time for myself,
and lead a less hurried existence. At the same time, I am
somewhat afraid of this, for two reasons. I'm afraid it isn't
possible—that it's unrealistic financially to buy a place of my
own in the country and that it's unrealistic professionally to think
I can isolate myself from "where the action is" and still write
successfully. I also have some fears about it actually coming
about. Suppose the opportunity presented itself and I moved.
Would it be as idyllic as I imagine? Would I get bored living out
in the country? What if my romantic fantasy of life as a country
gentleman is shattered by a much more harsh reality? What
then? What can I dream about?

I am reminded here of a line a friend has repeated to me
often: "Be careful what you ask for. You might get it." We can
dream and long for things much of our lives, afraid all the while
that we won't get them and also afraid that we will.

This is the neat little web of fear and anxiety many of us
wind ourselves into. Thinking through both sides of this and
talking about it with friends helps me. It makes me aware of the
conflicts, the fears, and the possible rewards. When I can free
myself of the tension, I can more readily open myself to other
possibilities: for instance, a home in the city and in the country,
swapping homes with someone for a while, living in the country
for one season and in the city for another. I can also take pressure
off myself when I realize that I don't need to make a clear choice
right now.

The whole point of this is to realize this link between our
fear and our desire. When we are conscious that something we

want badly is naturally going to be accompanied by fear, we can be better prepared to face the fears we have. When we see that some of the things we are afraid of hold something we are also drawn to, we gain a better understanding of our values and behavior.

A second theory I play with sometimes is a variation on Flip Wilson's "What you see is what you get"; it is: "What you fear is what you get." Sometimes this works in a self-fulfilling prophecy. I think it also has something to do with selective perception. The idea is that persons terribly afflicted by a fear behave in ways that draw to them the very thing they're afraid of. Fear is a magnet, a net that will wrap you up within itself.

Writers of the power-of-positive-thinking ilk have dealt with the same issue. The world has a way of delivering what you ask of it, they say. If you think you're going to fail, you will. Lack of faith in yourself cuts you off from the best parts of yourself and the world around you. Expect victory and you will get it.

This theory, that what you fear is what you get, works in my own attitude about myself in my professional life as well as in interpersonal relationships. Let's explore it.

One of the first things a good football coach teaches young players is not to play as if they're afraid of getting hurt. Because they surely will be. The coach might say something like this:

> Son, if you go out there and play like you're going to be hurt, you will be. If you slide into a tackle or turn away and wait for that guy to tackle you, you're gonna get creamed. You've got to put yourself—all you've got—into it every time. When you do it halfway is when you're going to get stomped on.

The analogy to life holds, I think. When we do something halfway and choose not to put our full energy and commitment into it, we are surely setting up its failure.

Let's take writing a book as an example. I am about to write a book and I am afraid of a hundred things—that I won't finish it, that I won't be able to sell it, that no one will read it, that someone will read it and think it's ridiculous. Any one of those alone could be enough to stop me from writing the book or, if I choose to go ahead and write it, could have me so preoccupied and tense that the book turns out a dismal mess.

Afraid of failing, I go into it predicting my own failure and, sure enough, it comes true.

The comment, "Yeh, I'll do it, but don't think it will work," reflects this. And as we saw in Chapter 6, one of my behaviors in this case, in order to protect myself, is not to give the project my total effort or to set very low standards for it. This way I can slough it off and save myself from giving my book an all-out, committed effort, and *then* face the possibility of failing. I am accepting a lesser punishment to avoid a greater one. The drawback is, of course, that by not risking a lot, I will not taste the fruits of high reward.

Yielding to your feelings of fear, consciously or not, is what perpetuates the "what-you-fear-is-what-you-get syndrome." If we can picture again how fear affects us physically and how we respond to the fear of failure, for instance, we can more clearly see how that sets up the very thing we fear. Tense, withdrawn, nervous, we hold ourselves back for the perceived danger. We set our sights low, if at all, and proceed with utmost caution. We pretend not to care what happens; to care would mean that we would be vulnerable. So we stay inside ourselves and suffer our worst fears.

There are two ways I see this working in personal relationships; one has to do with possessiveness, the other with the fear of rejection. I have experienced in my own life and seen all too often in others how the fear of losing a love partner contributes to that loss. One partner fears the loss of the other so much that he or she holds on much too tightly. "I need you so much that if you leave me I will die," is the message they give. This is the stuff of which love songs are made but in too many cases it leads to the strangulation of love, if any existed in the first place. A possessive partner often speaks out of insecurity. He or she is saying, in effect: "I don't have enough of myself so I need all of you, all the time, in order to fill me up." The more possessive one partner becomes, the more the other resists, until, desperate for freedom and his or her own growth, he or she bolts out of the relationship. An inordinate fear that I will lose you makes me behave in ways that contribute to you leaving me.

The fear of rejection has the same self-fulfilling quality about it. Most often my fear of rejection will lead me to be withdrawn. I will not offer many of my own opinions or say many personal things about myself. I will avoid telling you that I don't like something about you. Any of these could lead to an immediate put-down, something I couldn't stand. Most of the time, I do not have a very good opinion of myself and if you add yours to that it would wreck me. In this kind of relationship, the things that help glue people together, in a good way, are missing. Strong feelings, opinions about yourselves and the world, secrets shared, feedback, and healthy fighting all go by the board. Without those two people are like two shells, knocking on each other's hard exteriors. I fear rejection so much that I do not offer myself and therefore I am rejected.

One other way I see fear acting as a magnet is in an increased perception of the things one is afraid of. If I am afraid of moths, for instance, I look for them; I see many more of them than does someone who is not afraid of them. In the same way, when I am afraid of being rejected, I see many more cues that tell me that rejection is coming than does someone who is not afraid. The more cues I see, the more afraid I am and the more I withdraw. It is a tragic cycle because it plays itself out in so many lives and tears away at so many relationships.

The way out of the cycle takes the very things this person probably has little of—trust in himself as an individual and the courage to take risks in a one-to-one relationship.

Underlining all this, in a very important way, is an awareness, a sensitivity to our own feelings, fantasies, and needs. If I am not aware of myself, obviously I cannot go about meeting my needs and fulfilling the fantasies that mean the most to me. Several things may affect this awareness. If someone had gone most of his life having someone else constantly meet his needs, he might have a hard time being aware of what needs are his own and which are more important; further, he would probably have a hard time learning that he is ultimately responsible for meeting his own needs. Men brought up by doting mothers who depend on doting wives to keep them happy are good examples of this.

Conversely, a person used to having his needs and wants continually denied could conceivably be sorely out of touch with himself. A young man raised in an atmosphere in which his own needs were denied time after time might find it very painful to even be aware that he wants something badly. He is not used to getting what he wants and the fear of that happening again is too great for him to admit his own desires to himself.

Finally, the process of awareness is a confrontation with responsibility. When I become aware of something I want and fully admit it to myself, then I also know that I have reached a decision point. I can choose to ignore my want, rationalizing about it and telling myself it's not important. All the while, though, this tends to lower my opinion of myself; I am deceiving myself. Or I can choose to go after what I want, to take the risk involved and be responsible for my own success or failure. Knowing all this, many of us simply block out a full awareness of what we want in life to make us happy. After all, we reason, we probably won't get it anyway.

Again and again, this theme is repeated. This denial of self-importance springs out of fear. What do I want? is a much more important question than we realize. The answers may be covered up by years of meeting others' needs or "shoulds" from one authority to another. To begin to answer that question is to begin a journey of satisfying yourself, of meeting your own needs; it is moving toward responsibility. Perched on your shoulder as you go, tugging at your sleeve, and sometimes holding you motionless in its grip, is your fear.

What do you want? What are you afraid of?

CHAPTER 9

Sex, death, and surrender

Control. It is a watchword for our culture. Mastery of this. Command of that. Domination of them. Governing of those.

The ways we succeed and gain recognition in our society are by gaining and exercising control, over other people, institutions, and systems. We recognize and reward power, whether it is in politics, business, sports, or international relations.

"He really has things under *control*" is a high compliment indeed. We are "*master* craftsman" and "grand *masters*": we *master* our golf game, we score points for *controlling* our emotions, we *command* respect, we *govern* whole groups of people. We *dominate, rule, direct, restrain,* and *subdue*—nature, our children, our spouses, our employees, minority groups, and other nations. Those are the things we are rewarded for.

To control entails power, a sense that we have mastered

what will happen to us; we can guide the other people and other forces in our life to do what we need to be safe and secure.

On the other hand, losing control has a sense of shame and embarrassment. "I can't control those kids" is a statement reflecting frustration and a certain amount of shame. Many parents expect to be able to maintain control over another person's life not only through their childhood but well beyond the time the child is able to make responsible decisions for herself or himself. To lose that control is to "lose face."

"I can't help it, I just lost control" is an excuse, an explanation that we feel is needed to somehow explain undesirable behavior. Any sort of loss of control has a negative connotation—of people over whom you think you should have some degree of mastery, of situations you think you should be in charge of, or of urges or emotions you experience and expect to control. We are blamed, by others or ourselves, for losing control.

Similarly, the concept of surrender is unacceptable for most of us. We would rather suffer untold degrees of pain, financial ruin, the destruction of relationships, and even death before we surrender. The most recent example of this concept carried to absurdity in our national policy is the prolonging of our military involvement in Vietnam. As a nation, we preferred to spend billions of dollars and thousands of young men's lives rather than lose face in the eyes of the world by surrendering to the reality that existed in that country.

To yield or to give up goes against everything in the American ideals of winning, staying one up, and maintaining control. This concept permeates our culture. Obviously it affects each of us to different degrees, but in general this "requirement" robs us of a great deal. It is a source of much of the tension that ruins our heart muscle. It robs us of experiencing many of our emotions. It takes away spontaneity. It deprives us of many sensual pleasures. It steals away our orgasms and other peak experiences. And it is this fear of losing control that reinforces our negative and fearful attitude about death.

Washington Redskin football coach George Allen says, "Every time I lose, I die a little," and millions of Americans nod their heads in agreement. It's almost as if we believe that control or mastery of a situation gives us some kind of immortality. If we win, we live. If we lose, we die. We are the Christians in the arena with the lions, all over again, and we have to fight like hell to dominate the real and imagined lions of our life, lest we receive the thumbs-down signal from the emperor. If we capture and control, we go on as an active force, we live to fight again. If we surrender, we are pulled down into some dark, unknown undertow that carries us along, unwillingly, without any control, to . . . what?

I think if I had to name the one thing people were most afraid of, I could make a good case for the fear of letting go, of surrendering. Wrapped up in "letting go" is a loss of consciousness, an abandonment, a yielding to the forces within or outside of us. The fear of death and our not knowing what that means is very much a part of this fear of letting go. So are many of our sexual fears; we touch it when and if we are able to abandon ourselves to orgasm. We are too frightened to abandon ourselves, afraid of that ultimate surrender (at least we see it as ultimate), and yet perhaps it holds for us our most supreme joy.

My feeling is that sex and death have some things in common; we can make some enlightening analogies—that our fear of surrendering keeps us from in-joy-able sex, just as it keeps us from the in-joy-able process of living and dying. It is possible that we would enjoy the process of dying; many people who have thought they were dying or close to death have reported euphoric experiences and even pleasant sensations in their "final" minutes. More important to most of us, however (and more easily arguable), is how that fear of death, of surrendering, keeps us from yielding to who we really are while we're alive.

We constantly seem to want to control, accumulate, know, and keep, when perhaps the keys to a more joyful life are in giving away, letting go of control (liberating), becoming innocent again, and losing.

Imagine and believe, for the moment, that the act of sexual intercourse is an analogy for your life. The moment sexual feelings begin to stir inside is a moment of birth. The urges and feelings grow inside and eventually you act on them; they mature in a sense, just as we mature when we begin to act on our own feelings and take responsibility for them.

The physical act itself, from foreplay to climax and

dénouement, has a definite personality about it, the result of your own uniqueness and that of the person you're interacting with. You bring your own strengths and weaknesses to this act and to this meeting, your own way of being in the world is reflected in this coming together. You are master or slave or equal partner. You are aggressive, or passive, gentle or rough, demanding or accepting. You are relaxed or tense; you let go or you hold back. To these qualities, your partner adds his or her own, so that, in a physical way and in an emotional way, you either struggle and stall or you mesh and weave together a tapestry of complementary postures and feelings and parts of yourselves.

Throughout all of this runs the thread of control and surrender. How much do we let go? How much do we manipulate our partner? How much do we try and hold off our own desires, our own instincts, in order to do what we think is expected? When, if at all, do we surrender to the strongest feelings within ourselves and to the passions of the meeting? When, and how, do we come to that moment of most supreme joy? Is it born out of surrender or control?

Remember, we are imagining that this act of sex is an intense picture of our life and that we enter into it in much the same way and make the same choices, each of us in our own way. By looking at the sexual encounter as a microcosm of the way we are in the world, I think we can see more clearly how fear inhibits us and keeps us from what we want. If we can see the abandonment of the intense climax and the surrender to the most natural in ourselves as analogous to death, we can better understand how we avoid that surrender or prepare ourselves for it.

With that in mind, let's look at some of our sexual fears, our fears of death, and see how both are related to our need to control and our fear of surrender.

Because sex has been an area of such negativism in our culture, such a breeding ground for fear and guilt, it can be looked at as a boiling down, an intense distillation of the way fear holds us back and makes us reluctant to give ourselves permission to enjoy.

One of the most important ways we go about building a healthy self-image is to learn about, respect, and ultimately approve of our own natural self, including our natural sexual functions and the things that give us pleasure. The long list of taboos most of the society has against this process begins, at a very early age, to set up conflicts within children. What they want to do for themselves sexually is pitted against what we will allow them to do.

Natural, normal children want to explore parts of their own bodies, to stimulate themselves, to learn the differences between themselves and other children. They soon learn, from the models most influencing them, that sex is forbidden fruit, a curious mixture of pleasure and evil that only takes place at appropriate places at appropriate times; that you can do it when you gain some control over it; and that, most important, it is not something you enjoy with complete abandon. After all, it might control you.

So while the "no's" hammer in, the natural urges of the child struggle to be expressed. While first-hand experiences and the media tease him, the restraints of his parents' wishes hold him back. He is caught in our culture's pervasive double message on sex: yes-no, yes-no, yes-no. Yes to sex, to lure, to sell, to exploit, and yes to "normal" and "acceptable" sex, but no to exploring, to exposing our sexual feelings to each other, to being open and honest about it, to experimenting, God forbid, with things that give ourselves and others pure pleasure.

So our sexual behavior becomes a kind of surreptitious disobedience. The thoughts we have and the things we do are done behind closed doors and with the awareness that somewhere lurks a disapproving mother or father or God. Our sexual self becomes, then, a primary source for guilt, fear, and hostility.

One of the most powerful determinants of fear is the expectation of punishment. Any time we commit an act that we perceive as evil, we set ourselves up for the resulting fear of punishment. The more we feel judged, or the more judges and standards we have been submitted to in our history, the more possibilities there are for disapproval, for us to see ourselves as "evil"—and for fear. As we mature and make emotional and moral judgments for ourselves, we make a distinction between what was punishable to us as children and what we can do as adults without that punishment. Because sex is such a strong urge and also filled with so many taboos, judgments, and what we have come to see as evils, it is, tragically, filled with fears.

Karl Menninger, in his book *Man Against Himself*, writes about this fear of punishment as it relates to sex:

> A man married to a woman who unconsciously represents to him a new edition of the mother who successfully inhibited his sexual activities during boyhood could not possibly overcome this fear sufficiently to permit his body to act out his instinctive desires. The Hindu who sits on one foot for twenty years because he believes it to be his religious duty, could not possibly leap to his feet and begin to run, even if he were threatened by a fire or coaxed to a great reward.
>
> One is unconsciously dominated by childhood attitudes throughout life. In the normal person, the unfortunate misunderstandings of childhood are corrected by later experience, but it implies no weakness of intelligence that some persons cannot overcome them. The reactions of conscience are determined in early life and change but little as a result of experience. Accordingly, with or without the presence of conscious fears and quite independent of them, there exists in the unconscious of many people a compelling fear of punishment which is excited to great activity at the very moment when the ego believes itself threatened with an alluring temptation of a nature once associated with punitive pain, and the prohibition of this pleasure is, at the same time, a punishment in itself.
>
> How is this fear of punishment to be related to the wish for punishment with which we have met so frequently heretofore? I shall repeat what was said above: hysteria, of which impotence and frigidity are typical, indeed prototypical, is definable as a condition in which the function of the organ is surrendered to, modified—the purpose being the forestalling of anticipated injury to or the removal of that organ. Put in more familiar terms, the hysterical organ invites (wishes for) punishment of a lesser order to avoid punishment of a greater order.[1]

Thus a woman may say to herself, in the deepest part of her unconscious self: "I will not really enjoy this 'making love' with my partner. I will not abandon myself to the pleasurable sensations it gives me. And I will not let go and have an orgasm,

---

[1] From *Man Against Himself*, copyright, 1938, 1966, by Karl A. Menninger. Reprinted by permission of Harcourt Brace Jovanovich, Inc.

because if I do, I'll be severely punished for it. To avoid this punishment, I'll accept an unfulfilling sex life, I'll bear up to the sadness of that so I won't have to risk the disapproval, the rejection, the punishment that would surely come if I wallowed in the pleasure of making love."

Many other fears stand in the way of our complete enjoyment of sex. We are concerned with what is normal and abnormal. We are afraid we won't satisfy our partner. We are afraid we won't perform. We are afraid of being unresponsive. It is not the intent here to explore all of our sexual fears, but these that are expressed most often are worth looking into briefly. Again, we can see that some of the fears we have about sex relate to other areas of our lives as well.

Our fears about being normal come out in a number of ways. We may be afraid that we want sex too much—or not enough. It might be that what we want to do in our sexual behavior is not often done, in our perception, and would be disapproved of by most people or, worse, by our partner. Or we may be afraid that some aspects of our physical development, an injury or a physical handicap, will prohibit us from having sex "like everyone else does."

Any definition of normalcy is based on the values and practices of others outside of a relationship with you and any unhealthy fear about being normal is tied up with the feeling that the values of others are more important than your own.

Alex Comfort, in *The Joy of Sex*, had this to say about being normal:

> Tack "abnormal" onto a sexual taste and it becomes worrying. "Normal" implies that there is something which sex ought to be. There is. It ought to be a wholly satisfying link between two affectionate people, from which both emerge unanxious, rewarded, and ready for more. That definition includes the awareness that people differ wildly in what they need and in their capacity to be satisfied; more, statistically, than in almost any other measurable. Since sex is cooperative you can cater to one another alternately to bridge gaps. Add to this that sex, for reasons built into the species, makes us uniquely anxious compared with other divergences of need or taste and our culture is coming out of a period of moral panic into a reawareness that

there is nothing to fear. Accordingly, a lot of people are, in their sexual assumptions, like the generation of Victorian children brought up to believe that green sweets were poisonous and rice pudding was good for you because it was unpalatable; they need reassuring.[2]

We don't have a single "normal" pattern of sexual behavior, as Comfort points out. More appropriate questions, he says, are: "Why does this particular person need this emphasis (in his sex life)?" and "Is this behavior (a) spoiling his chances for being a full person, (b) tolerable for society?"

Size is another area we allow ourselves to get hung up on. A man is afraid his penis is too small to satisfy a woman. A woman is afraid her breasts are not big enough or that her vagina is too small. Or too big.

Rarely do any of our fears turn out to be justified when it gets down to actual sexual performance. But the fear is real, all the same, and often more than enough to keep the fear-affected man or woman from purely enjoying his or her sex.

The fear of impotence, of not being able "to get it up," runs rampant in men who have passed middle age. Studies by Kinsey and Masters and Johnson indicate that every man they surveyed over 40 expressed some degree of fear of not being able to get an erection sometime in his future, *even if he had never had such trouble.*

Sex researchers have found that age has nothing to do with impotency: disease does, obesity does, excessive use of alcohol and some other drugs does. But age does not affect a man's ability to achieve an erection.

Comfort points out in *The Joy of Sex* that all men are impotent sometime or another, for various reasons that are mostly not physical.

> If you can ever get an erection—by masturbation, in sleep or on waking—there is nothing physically the matter with the hydraulics. Age has nothing to do with impotence unless it brings illness. Belief that one is aging and must run out of steam has. Normal male potency lasts as long as life. The only change is that spontaneous erection gets rarer, direct skin stimulation is needed

[2] Taken from *The Joy of Sex*, edited by Alex Comfort, pp. 78–80. © Modsets Securities Ltd. Used by permission of Crown Publishers, Inc.

and orgasm takes longer to come. Impotence in old men is due to turn-offs, lack of health, and an attractive partner, attempts to perform too often, or the demands of a younger partner who sets them a proficiency test. These would turn normal people off at any age.[3]

Comfort, Masters and Johnson, Kinsey, and most other sex researchers agree that the fear of not being able to perform and satisfy a partner is the greatest single roadblock to a fulfilling sex life and the biggest reason older men do not continue to have sex.

Julius Fast, in his book *What You Should Know About Human Sexual Response*, underlines what we have said here in a single paragraph:

> Fear itself is a strong effect in actual failure. The fear that he will not achieve an erection will often cause a man to be impotent. Fear of losing an erection can cause it to be lost. Fear in general seems to be the greatest barrier to complete sexual enjoyment; fear of failure, fear of interruption, fear of the weakening effect of old age, fear of not satisfying a partner and fear that masturbation may have destroyed the ability to respond to a man or woman.[4]

Many sexual fears, particularly regarding men and impotency, have something to do with the high value our society places on being young and on performing. I believe it also has a lot to do with the particular mantle we have foisted on the American man, one he chooses to wear proudly. The qualities that we expect from men, especially in relationships, are initiative, aggressiveness, assertiveness, command, the ability to make the right moves at the right time. We have come to expect women to be passive, accepting, supporting, receiving, sympathetic, and reactive. These traits seem to be reflected in the physical act of sex as well as being qualities we look for in other interpersonal relationships.

For all too many men this station in life, this role they have grown into, is tied up—if not symbolized—by an erect penis, by the ability to always be ready to satisfactorily make love to a

---
[3] Ibid., pp. 243–44.
[4] Julius Fast, *What You Should Know About Human Sexual Response* (New York: Berkley Publishing Corporation, 1966), p. 106.

woman. When this is threatened or even perceived to be, it is not just an act of sexual intercourse that is threatened but a whole way of being in the world. After all, a man asks himself, how can I initiate anything, be assertive, aggressive and in charge, when, as it gets right down to it, I won't be able to perform?

Once threatened with experiences of impotency or even if the irrational fear becomes great enough, many men will withdraw from sexual activity completely rather than risk the earth-shattering, ego-destroying experience of failing in their basic nature at what everyone expects of them. We have placed, in this society, a very high value on male potency and along with that goes an inestimable amount of pressure on men, especially men with big egos. The more pressure, the more room for fear. The more fear, the greater potential for failure. Tragic paradox isn't it?

While this is the yoke many men are wearing, American women are caught in a double bind that is just as tragic. They are taught, essentially, to tease. Learning from role models in movies, magazines, television, billboards, and other media, they decorate themselves until they are an exhibit, but with a double message: yes but no, come on but stop, look but don't touch. Women are caught up with this double message not just to the men with whom they come in contact, but more important, from themselves to themselves.

The women with whom I come in contact who are changing this for themselves have first to get in touch with the fact that they have cut themselves off from their own bodies. The double message of "look but don't touch" that they have grown up with, in many cases, has not been just for men. The women themselves don't know how their bodies respond or what they like and dislike. They have been presented as objects, treated as objects, and they regard themselves that way.

Often the receptive, passive role we have hung on women makes them less-than-equal sex partners. Afraid of their own sexual desires, afraid to be "aggressive women," they hold back. They receive. They please their partner perhaps, but a full response to their own needs often goes by the boards.

All of us, in one way or another, reach out for contact with other humans. We need social intercourse. We crave the pleasure, the satisfaction, the sanity even, that human touch gives us. And we want the joy of sexual fulfillment. All the while the battle inside us rages—"I want to, but I shouldn't, it's not right." "I want to but I'm afraid I won't be good enough." "I want you but I'm afraid you won't want me." "I want to make love to you but I'm afraid I won't perform." "I want to let myself go with you, but I'm afraid I'll lose control."

In many ways we reinforce these fears and hold each other to the roles we have stepped into. When we keep someone else in that complementary role, we can stay safely in our own; we will not have to face the challenge of changing.

As the man is expected to perform in his own way, so is the woman. On top of the fear and guilt she may feel about inviting and enjoying sex, we expect her to be orgasic all, or most, of the time. If she has an orgasm, we males have "succeeded." It is seen as some reinforcement of the male role, some underlining of the qualities in men that they believe make them men. Perhaps it is that the male has succeeded in bringing his woman to surrender. The man operating, consciously or not, on this value system is missing something; as are the women who play into it.

Orgasm seems unique in our experience. We find it difficult to describe or to compare to other experiences we have. A total orgasm is a surrender. It is a letting go of consciousness, of control over our body, of our ego. It is the moment when we stand most naked and vulnerable and the moment when we are yielding to our most natural selves. As such, it can be laced with fear. In sex, as in life, to embrace these fears as part of ourselves and to transcend them is what allows us to move toward a fulfillment of all that we are.

In this quote from his book, *Total Orgasm*, Jack Lee Rosenberg summarizes briefly what happens in an orgasm and some of the fears it may bring:

> . . . the body starts off as a "thinking" entity, getting as much pleasure as it can from what the head, or ego, decides will be pleasurable. As the movements in intercourse or stimulation continue, and as the orgastic reflex takes over, movements begin in the pelvis and you get "out of control" (out of rational control). Gradually the movement direction shifts so that the forward thrust of the pelvis is made more and more from the ground or

feet. There comes a point of no return, after which the movement flows from the pelvis up to the head. Then follows a corresponding letting-go of the ego, when one completely flows with the melting quality of the orgastic reflex. For many people, a problem arises when, as the reflex action is ready to take over, a number of fears suddenly surface.

One of the fears you may experience in intercourse, as well as in other situations, is that, if you let go of your mind, you will "lose your mind"—go crazy. People who live entirely in their heads, thinking types, run the risk of getting stuck in their thinking process as an orgasm approaches, and turn off their sexual energies. Energy must flow freely in the body, because orgasm is a reflex reaction. It is as difficult to think yourself into a sneeze as it is to think yourself into an orgasm.

The fear of falling is another primary anxiety that can be triggered as an orgasm approaches. When you let your ego, or mind function, shift you do get a sense of falling. This can be very frightening. There also arises occasionally the fear of death. The association of death and orgasm is a common phenomenon. Reich saw the striving for nonexistence, for Nirvana, for death, as identical with the striving for orgastic release. This led him to believe that the orgasm is the most important manifestation of life. Reich cited two kinds of attitudes toward death and dying: either as an idea of severe injury or destruction of the psychophysical organism (in this case accompanied by severe anxiety and grouped around genital castration) or in the form of bodily dissolution, melting away, which is similar to full orgastic gratification and pleasure.[5]

". . . the striving . . . for death as identical with the striving for orgastic release." What is the curious link between orgasm and death? Many women report fantasies of dying and some existence after death during their orgasms. The French word for orgasm is "little death."

Are we, in the deepest part of ourselves, striving, as Reich suggests, for a full release from the tension, conflict, and tyranny some of us experience in the world we live in? Are we yearning, at some level, to die and transcend this life?

Some very disparate sources suggest that some of us, a very

---

[5] Jack Lee Rosenberg, *Total Orgasm* (New York: Random House, Inc. and Berkeley: The Bookworks, 1973), pp. 33–34.

small minority I'd guess, think of death in a different way. A bit of graffiti on a wall at San Francisco State University in 1970 proclaimed, "Death is the greatest kick of all, that's why they save it for last."

Socrates, when told that his end on this earth was near and he should prepare for his death, replied: "Know ye not that I have been preparing for it all my life?" He knew the best way to live his life was by fully facing the fact that it was going to end, that this final letting go is not something one prepared for in a final moment of courage and resolve. Sir Thomas Browne echoed this thought centuries later when he wrote that "the way to be immortal is to die daily."

If we look more closely at our fear of death, we can see how closely it relates not only to our sexual experiences but to many other opportunities in our life where we can let go and yield to a more natural, deeper part of ourselves.

David Cole Gordon has written a marvelous book called *Overcoming the Fear of Death*. What he has to say is so relevant here, I'd like to quote from him at length:

> One of the chief components of our fear of death is the unconscious fear of the cessation of thought. It is unconscious in the sense that it is rarely articulated: when we contemplate death, we hardly ever think of it in terms of losing our power to think, but we rather think of death as signifying the end of the bodily existence with which we are familiar.
>
> . . . people are afraid *not* to think. Most people think that meditation is concentrating on, and thinking about one object or thought. This is only preliminary to true meditation, which is not thought and no thinking. It is hard enough for most neophytes and apprentice Buddhas to concentrate on one thing at a time without requiring them to cease all thinking and thought. Many spend a lifetime meditating and never get beyond the point of being able to keep their focus on a single object or an idea for a slightly longer period than when they started. Most are terrified of not thinking and most of us are slaves of our own thinking apparatus and thoughts. There is nothing man fears more than cessation of his thoughts, which is his mind. Breaking his attachment to his mental apparatus is perhaps the hardest thing in the world for man to do, but perhaps the most vital if he is to change, flower, and become a new being.

The fear of death is really a conglomerate composed of the fears of time, decay, the unknown, irreversibility, the loss of pleasurable sensations, the loss of thought, and the loss of self. We have seen, and personal observation must confirm, that much of what we call life is really pain and suffering. It is self-evident that we would gladly relinquish that part of our life which we call suffering. It is also apparent that much of life falls into the neutral gray area which we call vegetative existing, where we are not conscious of anything much happening. In this state we are not conscious of either physical or psychological pain or pleasure.

We have seen that we have taken a measurement, which we call clock time, and permitted it to tyrannize over and control our lives. This mind-created convention, instead of being a convenience, has become a dictator that imposes fearful pressure and tension upon us insofar as we believe that, like sand, it is constantly slipping through our fingers, in spite of our frantic efforts to contain the grains by keeping our fingers tightly squeezed together. Once we see time for the imposter that it is, and see how we can confuse the measuring unit with the phenomenon which we are measuring, much if not all of our fear of time should be eliminated. While we are forced to live with conventional time insofar as it has imposed itself upon man, by the awareness of its essence we should at least be able to keep it in its place and not permit it to rule our lives.

We fear the unknown, decay, irreversibility, and transiency. Obviously, if the unknown becomes known, we no longer have any reason to fear it, and the condition of death is not as unknown to us as we think it is. But do we not live with the unknown all the time? Do we know what is going to happen the next moment which, even as we think of it, becomes now and the past? Do we know what lurks around the next corner, be it a literal or a figurative one? Do we know whom we will meet next, and what they will say? In this sense we are always living with the unknown. Why then should we be fearful of it?

We also fear that we will not persist in the same form we are now. We must accept the fact that there are many things we do not know and in all likelihood will not know. But we do know that there are periods in our life, of which we are presently amnesic, when we existed in the physical form with which we are most familiar. And is not life in all forms characterized by the cycle of birth, death, and rebirth and regeneration? Why should we fear what happens to us after death if we do not fear the state before our birth? Is this not relevant? And is not the question Who were we before our birth? important? What we really fear most, do we not? is the loss of our pleasurable sensations, our thoughts, our thinking ability and our self.

When one relinquishes his self, he lets go of his thoughts, self-consciousness, and the thought process, and he achieves unification. The unification experience is identical with the loss of the self. The loss of this pseudo self is precisely what is achieved in the moment of unification. Just as man reaches out for this experience, so he desires to be rid of the false self, which is an unconscious encumbrance in that it is insatiable and must be constantly nurtured; the more it is fed, the greater is its hunger. This self, as we have seen, is made up of shifting chimeras with no more reality than any other single, random, or stray thought. It is the self that obscures his real nature, and is the basic source of his existential anxiety, which represents fear of the future, regret over the past, and concern over the ever-elusive present. It is this anxiety which man calls unhappiness. This self, along with its creator, the thought process, is what prevents many from living and being truly alive; it identifies with the concept of living rather than with his vegetative existence, which he shares not only with animals and plants but with so-called inert matter.

Nor is this viewpoint anti-intellectual. Many of man's unification experiences can come through thought or mental activity. Intellectual insights and investigations have resulted in unification experiences, just as man's more physical activities have. Raja yoga, the way of the intellect, is recognized as just as traditional and valid a path to Nirvana as the physical hatha yoga techniques. We do not inveigh against the employment of the intellect, but rather against its chronic misuse, when it becomes, like time, a Golem or Frankenstein monster that tyrannizes its own creator. When this happens, man is even further alienated not only from himself but from his own mind as well.

Much of man's behavior is motivated by his desire for repetitive experiences of unification; between his fear of death and his desire for the unifying experience, a large part of his total culture can be explained. This culture includes his art, literature, books, motion pictures, drama, music, poetry, song, and comedy in addition to the sports and other activities we have discussed. Do not many of these forms give the reader, viewer, or watcher a vicarious unification experience? The experience may be vicarious insofar as one obtains it as an auditor, reader, or spectator, but it is just as real as one attained more directly. Are not literary and artistic works judged, albeit unconsciously, in large measure by the degree to which they can produce or evoke an experience of unity in man? Is not this, perhaps, the secret hallmark and universal standard we use to evaluate great works of art and great men?

Have we not seen that man's greatest happiness comes when he lets go of not only thought but the very process of thinking itself? Man is also fearful of letting go of the false or pseudo self that he has so carefully nurtured since his birth. This is a self composed of nothing but thoughts, but thoughts with a difference, the difference being that he has given these thoughts greater importance and significance by more constant reiteration than his other thoughts.

Are we not basically afraid of death because we simply do not know what it is, and because no reliable report has ever come back from the dead? But suppose we do know what death is. Would not this alleviate most of the terror associated with our finitude?

We do know what death is. Does not everything we know about the condition of death accord and conform with what we know about the experiences of unification? And is not this experience the one man most avidly seeks during his lifetime? Should he not welcome it when it comes? Is it not something that he is really quite familiar with, having tasted it many times during his lifetime? Why should he fear what is apparently a permanent condition and state of unification? The point of this book is that what we think we dread above all is really what we most desire. Death, which has frightened man since his emergence as a thinking creature, is his ultimate and eternal unification experience. Death comes to all, not as a scourge or punishment, but as the culmination and fulfillment of life.[6]

This lofty state of unification Gordon writes about and the abandonment of self to the pleasure of a total orgasm are not restricted to meditating yogis or to sex therapists and those under their tutelage. These are not out of the reach of ordinary men and women, yet too many of us have taken opposite paths. We

[6] David Cole Gordon, *Overcoming the Fear of Death* (New York: Macmillan Company, 1970). Copyright © 1969 by David Cole Gordon; reprinted by permission of Harold Matson Co., Inc.

have unlearned, in a real sense, what our natural selves knew when we were first naked, vulnerable, and unashamed of who we were.

A long and unyielding list of shoulds, judgments, and constant criticism, pressure to conform, a lack of love and respect—from within and without—for who we fully are—all these factors and more stand in the way of our unification, of our giving up ourselves to ourselves. We have separated our bodies, our minds, and our emotions and we have accepted a long list of controls that keep us in check and in tension.

We have come to not trust ourselves. Goethe said, "as soon as you trust yourself, you will know how to live." For most of us, this turns the idea of trust around. We grew up with the idea that trust is centered somewhere out there, in another person, in police, in governments; that we can trust others or we cannot and on that question depends so much of our behavior in the world.

We can reveal ourselves or not, we think, depending on how much we trust the person we're with. We can act affectionate or not, depending on how much we trust the man or woman we're with. But this idea turns it around. Trust is something you have for yourself, of yourself—much like love—and you give it away. By giving it away you gain it. Basic to the whole idea is to trust your own urges, your feelings, your wants for yourself, your hopes, your fears; know in your deepest heart that whatever goes on inside you is worthy.

This is a very liberating way to live, to surrender to yourself. You gain a belief in who you are and you can let go and simply be. You can give up the trappings and the phony postures of the false self who is constantly worried about what others will do or think. You can rely on your own instincts. What a wonderful gift we can give ourselves!

In exploring some of our sexual fears and relating them to our fears of death, I have tried to look with a different consciousness at two of the areas of our lives that are filled with the most dread and with the most potential for growth. What we have done, in our culture, with both sex and death, is put a cover on them. We have confined them to a pressure cooker of sorts and as long as they remain there, they will continue to subtly but powerfully control our lives. Just as we have with some institutions and individuals, we have deified sex and death; we have handed over too much of our power to them by wrapping them in cloaks of mystery and fear.

Through the experience of giving up to ourselves we can learn more about who we are. By losing control of our rational, should-thinking selves, we can come much closer to an understanding of what death is and what life is.

CHAPTER 10

Ways out

> *No one can advise you on something as delicate as your own machinery.*[1]
> ERNEST HEMINGWAY

It is very tempting to give advice. It seems so easy; I learn things for myself and I think I can help someone else by telling them what to do. Sometimes it can be so subtle. I start off by saying: "Now if I were you . . ." or "Well, most people I know would . . ." or "Here's what you should do."

But in the end it doesn't work. A person has to find out on his own. He has to do his own work and take his own consequences. This seems particularly true with regard to fear. I said in the introduction how many times I have wished I could give people courage, but known, at the same time, that it wouldn't have worked.

This is not an argument for standing alone and facing your fear by yourself. Asking for help, whether it's from a friend or a professional therapist, is admitting you're human and taking a

---

[1] Attributed by A. E. Hotchner, *Papa Hemingway* (New York: Random House, Inc., 1966), p. 62.

definite step toward responsibility for your dilemma. The kind of help you seek, it seems to me, is important. Advice is cheap. Insight, feedback, support, and care are invaluable.

Remember that fear can wrap you in a double bind. One can be afraid and afraid to be afraid; fearful of reaching out for help, afraid that the request will go unheard or be misunderstood or rejected. Fear may also lead you to take a friend's advice readily instead of deciding for yourself, or you may lean too hard on a therapist, substituting the process of talking about your problem for the act of taking responsibility for yourself.

All of this is kind of backing into saying that one of the temptations in a chapter like this is to say "Here are some answers for you." There are plenty of books in the how-to-master-your-fear department that promise answers; that even say "do this and you will be cured," as if it were a recipe. But I don't want to do that. This may be quibbling with words, but I don't talk much about "mastering" fears or "conquering" them. I believe in going with them, acknowledging them as a part of myself at this moment, and moving into them in my own way. Moving, accepting, growing, *because* of them, not in spite of them.

So what you may find in this chapter is a mixed bag—client-centered therapy, behavior modification, Zen, Gestalt, implosion therapy, personal experience—an ecumenical once-over of ways that some people use in dealing with fear.

Some generalities are in order. Obviously there's not much you can do about your fear if you're not aware you're afraid. Some of the descriptions of fear and physical effects in Chapters 2, 3, and 4 should help in that regard. Most of us have sublimated or kept a pretty tight cover on our fear, thus on our symptoms. Coupled with the fact that we have become pretty insensitive to our own bodies, we may not recognize when we are afraid.

If there are situations or people you consistently avoid or if you avoid doing new things in general, it may not be that you're specifically afraid of a person or situation but how you may be with them. Thus you can be afraid of spending an hour alone with someone because of what they may say or do to you, *or* because of some of your unexpressed anger, for example, that you're afraid to let them know about.

Awareness that you're afraid, then, is an important first step.

Acceptance is just as important. If you do not accept the fact that the fear is your own and that it's OK to be afraid, you will probably go through 101 avoidance trips that will keep you from doing anything about it. I like to acknowledge my fear openly. If there is no one else to tell it to, I can say it to myself, out loud. I can write about it. I can draw pictures of it. The point is, I can call it my own.

The third generality that comes to my mind in dealing with fear is a willingness to act. Unless there is a desire somewhere in me to grow, to push out my boundaries through the fear that is surrounding me, I will remain alienated from the fear and from myself.

Perhaps that's a strange way to talk about it . . . to be alienated from my fear. Again, the process I want to go through is of embracing my fears, not controlling them, not mastering them, but taking them in, respecting them, exploring them, making friends with them, in a sense. In that way I can grow in a way that I know is deep and lasting.

There is something about all this that speaks to me of wholeness. There is a sense of taking things, ideas, emotions, people into myself and growing bigger because of it. I have the notion that each alienated part of myself that I can bring "back home" makes me all the more unified and powerful. Fears, generally, can be things that we have alienated from ourselves because of unpleasant experiences in our past. Welcoming them back in can be a cause for celebration.

In this excerpt from Judith Wells' "Daddy's Girl," she describes an unusual way one person worked that out:

> I read someplace in many psychological readings, when I was trying to pinpoint my "problems," about a young girl in an African society. In her early teens, she was listless, lacked confidence and was fearful of males and masculine authority. Her tribe used a mode of transvestitism to exorcise her fears. She dressed up in the male military costume of the former colonial power of the area and began to dance in this costume. After the ceremony, the girl's confidence increased enormously, she no longer feared men, and she eventually developed into a mature,

self-reliant woman. The girl in this story acts out symbolically what the Little Girl must learn to do for herself; incorporate the authority, which she objectifies outside of herself, into her own person. She must develop a sense of her own personal authority and hence self-approval. When the Little Girl develops this sense of self-approval, she will no longer be a Little Girl, but a mature woman—a full, complete human being.

A large part of the alienation we have from our fears, thus from ourselves, occurs because we leave things like power, acceptance, love, and authority outside ourselves. We are so used to depending on or looking to others for those things as children that we continue to look for them from others as we grow older. The process of maturing, of becoming whole, is one of taking these qualities inside one's self and owning them—responsibility for self, acceptance of self, love of self—the discovery and acting out of the reality that we are fully functioning adults who can be and do whatever we want.

My first task then is to welcome my fears back, to know that this is a stimulus to growth, to look at this act as a forward step on the road to becoming unified.

In some of the methods that psychologists, psychiatrists, and specialists in human behavior use, there are some clues as to what our fears are and how we might turn them to our own use.

Behavior therapy, or behavior modification, has become very popular and though it has been criticized for what some think are mechanical, impersonal methods, many of the therapists working with it have achieved considerable success.

Basically, as the name implies, it deals with a person's behavior and the present stimuli for that behavior rather than the reasons rooted in the past or the original stimulus. Behavior therapy, in general, asks the question "How?" rather than "Why?"

Inappropriate behavior, or behavior that is harmful or limiting to a person has been learned and can be systematically unlearned with a more beneficial behavior taking its place. The idea is that the stimulus—a person, an animal, or a situation—that caused the undesirable behavior in the first place is no longer available to the person to be dealt with. The present stimulus that reminds or duplicates the original fear, or anger, or hurt is available and can be dealt with, accompanied by the support and insight of the therapist.

Behavior therapy can be and has been used to deal with sexual problems, alcoholism, obesity, and bed-wetting, but it has been most widely used in the treatment of irrational fears. Sessions usually begin with the persons imagining and expressing the things they are most afraid of—elevators, bridges, horses, driving, crowds, pollution, etc. They are sometimes asked to talk about the worst situation they could imagine relative to their fear; others are asked to make a list of specifics, often in rank order.

If the fearful person begins to become anxious during this expression, the therapist begins to direct him or her to gradually relax, talking in an almost hypnotic way, trying to relieve the tension that accompanies the imagined fear. This process, sometimes called "systematic desensitization," takes patience and time in the therapist's office as well as homework. The ultimate aim is to have the fearful person gradually be able to relax as he imagines or experiences the things he is afraid of.

For instance, if you were afraid of crossing bridges, a behavior therapist might have you imagine yourself seeing a bridge at some distance, then driving toward the bridge, stopping at the beginning of the bridge, then driving on and perhaps being stalled in traffic on the bridge. At each step he would help you consciously work on relaxing the tension in your body until you could go on to the next step. At the end you might imagine yourself standing on the bridge alone in a high wind.

An obvious extension of this is to have direct exposure to the source of your fears, therapy "in vivo," so to speak. An example of this kind of therapy is found in the case of Robert, an eight-year-old San Diego boy who became frightened of school. Robert was intelligent, high-strung, and fairly sociable, but after an extended and rather serious illness, he could not bring himself to return to school.

Despite repeated and patient efforts by his parents, his teachers, and the school principal, Robert panicked when he thought he was going to have to go to school in the morning. Often he had physical symptoms such as extreme nervousness and vomiting.

Six months of traditional psychotherapy, which lasted from the spring through the following fall, failed to bring Robert around. On the first day of school in the fall he lost his nerve and wouldn't leave the house.

Robert's therapist decided to try behavior therapy and began a systematic program of a gradual return to school without much further attention to the reasons Robert felt so afraid. The first day Robert and the therapist took a ride, passed the school, and returned to sit outside at the curb. The following day they both stepped out of the car and walked across the street to the curb. The next day they walked across the sidewalk and up to the school steps. Whenever Robert said he was beginning to be afraid, he and the therapist returned immediately to the car, where Robert was praised for going as far as he had.

It took nineteen days to have Robert feel comfortable in the school. On the twentieth day, the therapist stepped out of the picture and Robert was accompanied to class by the principal. Robert opened the classroom door, walked to his seat, and began his work. Since then he has had no difficulty remaining in school.

In New York, Dr. Manuel Zane, a former psychoanalyst who has turned to behavior therapy, took a "class" of nine of his patients who were terrified of elevators through an experience he designed just for them. Dr. Zane did not go through the usual relaxing exercises, but took his patients to a downtown building where they took a quick course on elevators. A representative from Otis Elevator Company took the group on a tour of the workings of an elevator, above and below ground. Patients found out exactly what made it work and what could go wrong and what couldn't. Some of them were relieved when they learned that the elevator couldn't possibly lose control and crash through the roof.

During the "class" Zane's patients were constantly monitoring and talking about their fear levels. He even had them assign ratings, from 1 to 10, to the things they were afraid of. They talked amongst themselves, to the man from Otis, and to Zane—about the things that were right in front of them—the elevator buttons, the doors, the hatch at the top—anything that was in the present. At the end of a ten-week session, each of the nine people involved in the program was riding the elevator alone.

The principles used in behavior therapy can be used by the ordinary person for everyday fears and anxieties and it is applicable whenever there is a set of disturbed feelings evoked by an identifiable stimulus. The idea is to gradually expose yourself to situations, people, or things you are afraid of, step by step, with support each step of the way. Information helps immensely; that is, the more you know about the person or situation, the easier it will be for you to move ahead.

Let's take an example. It's my experience that many of us are afraid to be angry. There could be many reasons for this—we have no good models for our anger, we have been punished for being angry, "nice girls" aren't angry, the person we're with doesn't handle anger well, we're afraid of rejection if we're angry, and so on.

But being angry is human and it is unhealthy and self-defeating if we hold it inside or turn it on ourselves. Joan knows this and still she's afraid to be angry. How might she get past this fear of her own anger using some of the lessons of behavior therapy?

First, Joan might imagine herself getting angry. She might picture herself talking back to her husband and telling him in an honest and direct way about something she's angry about. She could picture herself shouting at him, really letting him have it, venting all the anger she's been holding in.

As she pictures this, she would be conscious of her body, sensing when she becomes tense and fearful. Then she could take steps to relax and let the experience seep into herself and be accepting, at least in her fantasy.

Then she might take a further step and tell her husband about her fantasy and what it was like for her. Here, her relationship with her husband becomes extremely important and the whole experience could become a negative one if Joan and her mate are not used to expressing feelings to each other or don't communicate well. It is one thing to try and walk through your fears in a supportive atmosphere, such as with an understanding friend or with a therapist, and another to walk into the dragon's cave, if that's what it is.

Assuming this experience is a good one, Joan, after taking these two steps, could really congratulate herself and perhaps receive some support from her husband for doing something she has been afraid of. This frees her to take more steps. She and her husband might decide to seek some help in achieving a more open communication with each other, moving to a place in their relationship where they can help each other do things they have been fearful of.

This is a big part of what a good relationship is about, to me. I want to be able to nurture the hidden, or just blossoming parts of my partner's personhood. I want to be able to provide the support and patience another person needs—and to get that for myself—so that we can both move through the fears and blocks keeping us from becoming all that we want to be.

Sometimes I have this picture of a person wearing a suit—his potential—that is too big for him. I want to be able to grow into that suit and to help others as well. To the extent that we can face our fears, we will have gone a long way.

If Joan, then, can identify and begin to nibble away at something she has been feeling but afraid to act on, she will have taken a very important step in her own personal growth and a step toward improving her relationships with others.

During this, or even before she starts, it would help Joan to find out what she can about anger. She might read articles or books about it, ask some friends about how they experience anger, talk to a counselor about it, or attend a seminar on anger or open communication.

In this example, Joan has taken some principles from behavior therapy and helped herself. That's generally what it's all about anyway. Behavior therapy is a term that we human beings have invented that means simply paying attention to and helping the way we act.

Joan has become aware of her feelings and that she is not acting the way she would like. She identifies her feeling specifically: she is afraid to get angry. She picks out one area: she is afraid to get angry at her husband. She learns something about anger and, in the process, herself. Then she takes some steps that bring those fears out into the open, where she (and her husband) can deal with them. Along the way, she takes her time, gives herself support or seeks it elsewhere, but keeps moving toward what she wants.

Again, as far as this kind of help is concerned, there is no active need to know the original reason for your fear or to dwell on your relationships with people in your distant past, as there is in Freudian therapy. It does not take as long as more traditional therapy either, and therefore tends to be less expensive. Some professionals, for these reasons and others, think that behavior modification is superficial, a quick once-over that deals only with symptoms, and that, once treatment is over, some other stimulus will appear to take the place of the one that has been "erased."

Many practitioners of behavior therapy, however, are proving through follow-up studies that in many cases it is thorough and effective and will get results where traditional analysis has failed.

Implosive therapy takes this whole idea one step further. It is more confrontive, less supportive, and encourages persons in therapy to face their worst fear directly.

Implosive therapy is based on the same principles we have just discussed, that fear is learned from experiences that have brought up punishment, frustration, and pain, and that it can be unlearned or "extinguished."

The therapist coaxes the patient into fantasies of his worst fears; step by step the imaginings become more terrible, more gross. Perhaps the patient experiences these almost as waking nightmares and his body trembles with anxiety or he becomes numb and listless. The therapist moves on, suggesting scenes designed to take the patient, in his own mind, to a hell of his own making. The therapist is there all the time, but there is little support offered; the patient is encouraged to go it alone.

In the February 1975 issue of *Psychology Today*, therapist Thomas G. Stampfl described his treatment of a patient named Leonard who was obsessive about cleanliness. Leonard washed his hands between fifty and one hundred times a day. One of the stimuli, identified early in the therapy, was a wastebasket. Here is part of Stampfl's description of part of one therapy session:

> According to the principle of extinction, the more Leonard imagined that [previous] scene, the less anxious he should feel

about wastepaper baskets. This was the case. But I wanted to get at the more deeply avoided stimuli that made wastepaper baskets repellent to Leonard in the first place. At our 11th session, I described, as vividly as I could, spit, mucus, vomit, and guano dripping from Leonard's hands. "Imagine the greenish, yellowish, shimmering grain of the mucus," I told him. "Imagine the soft, chocolate mushiness of the guano."

In a later session, I dwelled on the lump in Leonard's throat. I told Leonard the lump was guano. "Imagine that lump going down inside you, eating out your stomach lining, your heart, your other internal organs [Leonard had complained of pains in these areas]." This imagined scene provoked a marked reaction in Leonard. He began to gurgle softly. His gaze went glassy. His body grew rigid. I dwelled on the scene for five to ten minutes, until his anxiety diminished and he returned to normal.

The therapy went on like this and eventually Leonard was rid of his compulsion about being clean. Stampfl, while admitting that it is controversial, says implosion therapy is very effective and improves the patient's life. He calls it "staring down your nightmares."

If it is an apt analogy that behavior therapy helps you make mudpies of your fears and play with them, then implosive therapy would have you wallow in the mud—or at least imagine it—until you are no longer afraid.

Client-centered therapy, while it acknowledges some of the same truths about fear and human behavior, is different from either of the above. The premise in client-centered, or person-centered, therapy is that the person asking for help is his own best resource, that the answers lie inside him and, with support, feedback, and an increasing sense of personal power, he can find his own answers and act on them. It is much less directive or probing than some other forms of therapy and places an emphasis on the interaction between the counselor and patient more than on events outside the space and time they are together.

Rather than direct you to steps or suggest exercises, a "pure" client-centered therapist would help you in devising your own ways out, if you wanted to. Rather than lead you into an exploration of the relationship you had with your mother or father, he might suggest you share your feelings you have about your wife, yourself, or him. Rather than tell you what your problems are, he will encourage you while you define your own.

One of the primary objectives of the person-centered therapist, in my view, is to help a person establish a personal power base. There is an emphasis on realizing what you do to and for yourself, learning to trust yourself, realizing what you do to give away power, and gaining responsibility for your own actions.

Because client-centered therapy is so keyed to the present needs of the person being counseled, it is difficult to cite examples that would hold up as "typical." However this description, by the founder of client-centered therapy, Carl Rogers, gives us a good idea of the beliefs behind it and a hint of what it might be like to be involved in it.

> If the therapy were optimal, intensive as well as extensive, then it would mean that the therapist has been able to enter into an intensely personal and subjective relationship with the client—relating not as a scientist to an object of study, not as a physician expecting to diagnose and cure, but as a person to a person. It would mean that the therapist feels this client to be a person of unconditional self-worth: of value no matter what his condition, his behavior, or his feelings. It would mean that the therapist is genuine, hiding behind no defensive façade, but meeting the client with the feelings which organically he is experiencing. It would mean that the therapist is able to let himself go in understanding this client; that no inner barriers keep him from sensing what it feels like to be the client at each moment of the relationship; and that he can convey something of his empathic understanding to the client. It means that the therapist has been comfortable in entering this relationship fully, without knowing cognitively where it will lead, satisfied with providing a climate which will permit the client the utmost freedom to become himself.
>
> For the client, this optimal therapy would mean an exploration of increasingly strange and unknown and dangerous feelings in himself, the exploration proving possible only because he is gradually realizing that he is accepted unconditionally. Thus he becomes acquainted with elements of his experience which have in the past been denied to awareness as too threatening, too

damaging to the structure of the self. He finds himself experiencing these feelings fully, completely, in the relationship, so that for the moment he is his fear, or his anger, or his tenderness, or his strength. And as he lives these widely varied feelings, in all their degrees of intensity, he discovers that he has experienced himself, that he is all these feelings. He finds his behavior changing in constructive fashion in accordance with his newly experienced self. He approaches the realization that he no longer needs to fear what experience may hold, but can welcome it freely as a part of his changing and developing self.[2]

Gestalt therapy is a bit more stylized, a bit more focused on certain ways of dealing with people than Rogers' client-centered therapy. Founded by therapist Fritz Perls, Gestalt is primarily concerned with the closing of open wounds, the finishing of incomplete life situations, the removal of emotional "blocks" and the things a person consistently avoids.

Above all, Gestalt is grounded in awareness; the therapist relies heavily on a moment-by-moment awareness of what is going on in the person seeking help and that person, in turn, is encouraged to be acutely aware of his or her own feelings.

This, from Perls' *Gestalt Therapy Verbatim*, is a partial description of Gestalt:

> These are two legs upon which Gestalt Therapy walks: *now* and *how*. The essence of the theory of Gestalt Therapy is in the understanding of these two words. *Now* covers all that exists. The past is no more, the future is not yet. *Now* includes the balance of being here, is experiencing, involvement, phenomenon, awareness. *How* covers everything that is structure, behavior, all that is actually going on—the on-going process. All the rest is irrelevant —computing, apprehending, and so on. . . .
>
> The great error of psychoanalysis is in assuming that the memory is reality. All the so-called traumata, which are supposed to be the root of neurosis, are an invention of the patient to save his self-esteem. . . . They are all lies to be hung onto in order to justify one's unwillingness to grow.
>
> Freud devoted his whole life to prove to himself and to others that sex is not bad, and he had to prove this scientifically.

---

[2] Carl R. Rogers, *On Becoming a Person* (Boston: Houghton Mifflin Company, 1961), pp. 184–85. Reprinted by permission of the publishers and Constable & Company, Ltd., London.

In his time, the scientific approach was that of causality, that the trouble was *caused* by something in the past, like a billiard cue pushing a billiard ball, and the cue then is the cause of the rolling of the ball. In the meantime, our scientific attitude has changed. We don't look to the world any more in terms of cause and effect: We look upon the world as a continuous on-going process. We are back to Heraclitus, to the Pre-Socratic idea that everything is in a flux. We never step in the same river twice. In other words, we have made—in science, but unfortunately not yet in psychiatry—the transition from linear causality to thinking of process, from the why to the how.

If you ask how, you look at the structure, you see what's going on now, a deeper understanding of the process. The *how* is all we need to understand how we or the world functions. The *how* gives us perspective, orientation. The *how* shows us that one of the basic laws, the identity of structure and function, is valid. If we change the structure, the function changes. If we change the function, the structure changes.[3]

Perls' way of dealing with people he was counseling was to doggedly frustrate their attempts to rationalize or excuse their behavior. He would consistently work to a person's impasse or block and, through a process of feedback and confrontation, bring that person to his own awareness of the behavior that was holding him back.

Fear is very much a part of the work in Gestalt therapy. Perls continually talked and wrote of "catastrophic expectations," "risk taking" and, as in the above quote, a person's "unwillingness to grow." What a person repeatedly avoids—or is, at some level, afraid of—represents a hole, an incompleteness, *a void*. The healthy drive to authenticity then is to complete, to fill in these voids, to round out our whole selves.

Perls would ask the question: "What are you avoiding?" that might include behavior that was phobic, prolonged confusion, fixation on irrelevant issues, withdrawing of attention, or being insensitive to what was happening right in front of you. Once you become aware of your *a void dances* you take on the responsibility for changing your behavior.

[3] Fritz Perls, *Gestalt Therapy Verbatim* (Moab, Utah: Real People Press, 1969), pp. 43–44.

Let's move our attention for a moment to Zen, a jump that is not as far as you might think. Perls' writing and work, as well as those of other existentialists, is sprinkled with references to Eastern thought. In particular, Perls dealt with what in Zen is called *Maya*, a state of illusion that exists between your awareness of yourself and your awareness of the world; it is kind of a hazy middle ground in which the ego becomes too involved and a real awareness of yourself or your world in the here and now is prevented. To the extent that we exist in that *Maya*, we are out of touch with reality.

To practitioners of Zen, that is the fate of most people in the West. We are wrapped up, invested in, illusions of ways things should be and ways we want them to be instead of the way things *are, now*.

In the introduction to the book *The Three Pillars of Zen*, Huston Smith writes of the relevance of Zen to us:

> We understand the specific attraction of Zen Buddhism when we realize the extent to which the contemporary West is animated by "prophetic faith," the sense of holiness of the *ought*, the pull of the way things could be and should be but as yet are not. Such faith has obvious virtues, but unless it is balanced by a companion sense of the holiness of the *is*, it becomes top-heavy. If one's eyes are always on tomorrows, todays slip by unperceived. To a West which in its concern to refashion heaven and earth is in danger of letting the presentness of life—the only life we really have—slip through its fingers, Zen comes as a reminder that if we do not learn to perceive the mystery and beauty of our *present* life, our *present* hour, we shall not perceive the worth of *any* life, or *any* hour.[4]

One of the "koans" of Zen (a koan might be called an attitude or basic belief) is that the present moment, just as it is, is the reality of our ideal world. Nothing exists except the here and now.

From this basic tenet grows the emphasis of *awareness* in Gestalt therapy, the focus on *process* in Rogers' client-centered therapy, the attention to the present *behavior* in behavior

---

[4] Huston Smith, introduction to *The Three Pillars of Zen*, ed. Philip Kapleau (New York: John Weatherhill Inc., 1965).

modification, and the moment-by-moment feedback in encounter groups. We live now. We carry burdens and treasures from our past, we hold hopes, fears, and shoulds out in front of us, but we *live* now. It is the devotion to the here and now, and only that devotion, which allows us to face ourselves and take responsibility for our own lives. It is the devotion to the here and now that allows us to face our fears and move to a wholeness, a unity by filling out our *a void dances.*

This limited review of several different kinds of therapy is meant for you to draw some of the central ideas from some of the ways people are helping other people grow. Some are recent; some are centuries old. In the context of this book, I am trying to draw from these different types of therapy, ways you and I can meet and deal with our fears.

In each of these I find a strong sense of the regaining of responsibility. In observing or counseling a fearful person, as well as from an "interior" view—the person's view of himself—there is the feeling that the responsibility for what happens to his life is in the control of outside forces. A woman is afraid of what her husband will do to her, a boy is afraid of his teacher, a man is afraid of what his boss will do. We are afraid of an economic depression, a war, our marriage breaking up, and a host of other things. (You fill in your own fears.)

Some of the reasons for these fears relate to the fact that we are enmeshed in a society wherein we feel little control over what happens. As we feel less and less of a voice in the social and political matters that affect us, we feel more and more powerlessness, more and more fear.

Fear is bred in a vacuum of information and power. This holds true of a national government and a one-to-one relationship. If we feel incapable of influencing our government's policy on the Middle East, energy, or the recession, we are more afraid of what will happen. When we feel less informed as to what our options and alternatives are, we are more afraid. When we give away or have taken from us the information and responsibility around key decisions in our lives, we become afraid. When we let a spouse make most of the decisions about our relationship, we can more easily be afraid of what he or she might decide.

Picture a person who has given away most or all of his/her

responsibility to other persons or institutions—parents, spouse, boss, news media, city government, President, best friend. Such a person is not only fearful of what others will do to him or her, but wrapped in resentment and anger over all the "wrong" decisions that are being made about his/her life. Fear keeps us from taking responsibility for ourselves because we are then faced with the real task of guiding a real human being through the only life we have and taking the consequences. It seems easier for many of us to blame others or make excuses.

The personal regaining of this responsibility is a liberating experience. That may sound paradoxical at first, that being responsible is freeing, but not if we are responsible only for ourselves. Along with that great body of persons who are willing to let others be responsible for them, there is seemingly an equal number willing to take responsibility for others—the fathers and mothers of the world who want to take care of everyone, but don't take care of themselves—you undoubtedly have one or two in your life. The fears and resentments raised in this kind of people are just as bad, if not worse, than in those persons who will not be responsible for themselves. When I take responsibility for others I can be afraid not only of what will happen to me, but afraid for you as well.

A big part of moving through your fear then is to accept responsibility for yourself and only yourself. It means choosing, making hard decisions, accepting consequences, getting rid of excuses, and blaming no one.

That responsibility goes right along with the notion I expressed as very much a part of client-centered therapy—that of building your own personal power base. Various therapists talk about it in different ways: mobilizing your own resources, gaining your own strength, or becoming more assertive. Training courses in self-assertion, particularly for women, are becoming more and more popular as individuals realize how much we have given away our power to others. We are learning what it means to deny who we are to the world by consistently repressing our feelings, putting off meeting our needs, and avoiding the choices that present themselves to all of us.

Recognizing this in your everyday life may prove a bit difficult. Again, it's awareness. Some of us have become so used to patterns of behavior that it would be difficult to recognize the things that are keeping us from what we want. We may not feel that little twinge inside when someone else decides something for us and we don't say anything. Then again, we may feel it, down there in our stomach, and be afraid to say anything about it.

To assert yourself, simply, is to affirm your own existence, to recognize and speak for the ideas, feelings, wants, needs, hopes, and fears that are yours. It is the beginning of building your own power base.

Another thing in common expressed in differing kinds of therapy is a process of getting to know your fear. You'll remember that in systematic desensitization fears were listed and described. In implosion therapy the therapist and patient explored the worst imaginable fears in vivid detail. Then there were the patients in New York who visited and examined the object of their fears, the elevator.

All these are ways of coming a little closer to your fears and realizing that they are not so harmful after all. The idea is to squarely face whatever it is you are afraid of, examine it, turn it around in your hands, look at it from as many sides and in as many ways as possible, ask what makes it work, and observe how you interact. You can do this with an elevator or a person, an airplane or a cocktail party. The more information you have collected about whatever it is you are afraid of, the more options you have. You can choose, based on your own needs, rather than be controlled through your fear.

Through all of this flows the theme of here and now—this moment, no other. Awareness and the here and now go hand in hand. I can only be aware of my feelings now, not an hour ago, and not two days from now. I can remember or I can predict, but either of those things have little to do with my own responsibility, my own sense of power in this very moment. When we are afraid, we are afraid of what will happen *if*—we are afraid because of some experience in the past that has taught us and we are predicting that it will happen again. Remember from Chapter 2 how easy it is for us animals to generalize, to take one negative experience and apply it to all similar experiences? We think we are good at generalizing and predicting, even when our fear of what will happen to us deprives us of what we want most.

We have gotten so used to living in the future, counting on that goal we have, worrying about how we will meet it, and wondering about what others expect of us that our lives are filled with tension and fear. We have to meet deadlines. We have to face a person we don't like tomorrow. We have to earn $1000 by the end of the month. Each of these expectations takes us out of the present, out of the only moment we really have. We are projected into that fantasy realm Perls and Zen practitioners call Maya, where we wallow in anxiety over the terrible ills that await us.

In terms of our personal growth, we cannot move on until we are attentive to the present moment. There is no real "moving on," to leave conflicts, and unresolved situations behind. The anger, the fear, the frustration we have stays within us unless it is expressed or satisfied in some way. It holds onto our energy and will subtly control us, popping up again and again, perhaps at different places, but it is the same old fear nevertheless.

Fear is that one emotion which dooms us to repeat our mistakes of the past. Because we have been hurt we will carry it with us, afraid to be hurt again, and live out the self-defeating patterns our fear of pain sets up—unless we take the wherewithal to face what it is we are afraid of.

We cannot change the past. We cannot truly deal with the future. The only moment we can give ourselves to is now. We cannot forget our fears; nor can we really predict, even in the next moment, what love or pain will come to us. But we try. We hold onto old hurts and predict new ones, and fear, that mysterious, haunting, ever-present dark cloud, pervades our past, present, and future time and waits to be embraced.

CHAPTER II

The new

"What do you want to be when you grow up?"

Remember that question and how many times smiling adults would squat down close to your face and, with a wink to your Mom, ask it? I had a ready answer when I was seven: "An ice cream man." There was nothing I could dream of that would be better than roaming my old neighborhood ringing that Pavlovian bell, driving that shiny white truck with an unlimited supply of Good Humors and Popsicles packed in dry ice behind me. It seemed to me that the ice cream man went through his 40-hour week making kids happy, spreading good humor, if you will.

When I was ten, I was a bit more of a smart aleck. I answered: "a man." Adults didn't like that much because (1) it seemed like a smart-aleck answer and, (2) it sounded too vague, not very ambitious, and nonprofitable. Nonetheless, it was honest.

Then as I moved into adolescence, the ice cream man and the just plain man were replaced in rapid succession by a host of baseball and football players that swung at me, threw to me, and leaped head-first at me from bubble gum cards. I wanted to be Mickey Mantle and Johnny Unitas and spent days and days of my youth emulating them.

Later on I decided I wanted to be a cartoonist and I sent away for a pliable wooden doll that would serve as my model and a kit that would mold me into a best-selling graphic artist. The correspondence course promised fame and fortune when I learned to tickle the funnybone of the American public and I had visions of slaying social ills with the sweep of my India-ink-filled pen. Alas, Charles Schultz or Herblock I was not.

Then came a turning point, a day of decision. In the Spring of my year in the ninth grade at Thomas Jefferson Junior High School we had a "career day." All the young men and women in the social sciences class made up their minds then and there what they wanted to be. My decision seemed very important to me at the time and I remember feeling relieved when I had finally made up my mind. I would be an engineer. The country needed engineers (remember Sputnik?). There would be a demand for my services. I could find a secure job, and I would make a lot of money.

The American Dream revisited—making others happy. Fame as a "superstar": success, money, security. Don't gloss over those familiar words quickly. They represent what most of us have bought as our purpose in life. They are what motivate all too many of us, give our existence meaning.

What is it that you want to be when you grow up? Let's keep asking the question. Let's not believe for a moment that we are fully forged persons on our twenty-first birthday. Or our sixty-first. Let's acknowledge—celebrate, in fact—the notion that we keep changing and growing, if we are lucky, until we reach the grave.

Most of us are just beginning to learn, in an academic way, what many of the more fortunate among us have known for a long time: that there are stages of adult growth too and that the evolution of our personality continues at least through our sixtieth year.

As Roger Gould, of the UCLA department of psychiatry, said in *Psychology Today*:

> Like a butterfly, an adult is supposed to emerge fully formed and on cue, after a succession of developmental stages in childhood. Equipped with all the accouterments, such as wisdom and rationality, the adult supposedly remains quiescent for another half a century or so. While children change, adults only age.

Not so, Gould emphasizes, and goes on:

> Childhood delivers most people into adulthood with a view of adults that few could ever live up to. A child's idealized image of an adult can become the adult's painful measure of himself. Without an active, thoughtful confrontation of this image, the impression of childhood will prevail. An adult who doesn't undertake this thinking and this confrontation lives out his or her life controlled by the impossible attempt to satisfy the magical expectations of a child's world.
>
> The process of change means coming to new beliefs about oneself and the world.[1]

"New beliefs." "Active, thoughtful confrontation." Change. Where does it all lead? How do we continue to grow? How can we direct that? How does fear get in the way?

The question takes on a larger meaning: What do you want to be when you grow up? I want to keep growing. I want to become whole.

That is my meaning, that is the construct I put around my daily experiences, the net of purpose I can fall back into when I feel weak or alone or needing. I can say it in different ways—self-actualization, living up to my potential, knowing myself, realizing all that I am. Whatever the term used, the concept has a meaning for me at a real feeling level as well as being something I can think about and talk about.

I believe I move toward that wholeness in two ways:

---

[1] Roger Gould, "Growth Toward Self-Tolerance—Adult Life Stages," *Psychology Today*, February, 1975, p. 78.

learning and loving. My unique wholeness is my goal; learning and loving are the process. To learn is to take in, to grow, to change, to live. To love is to give, to trust, to risk, to invest in the unknown. There is a neat duality there that appeals to me—taking in through learning and giving away by loving or nurturing. I am, ideally, constantly expanding my own perimeters, moving out my own limits as I take in nourishment, and I am repeatedly giving myself away, knowing that there will be more where that came from.

Against this backdrop let's examine the role fear plays in gumming up the things I believe we want most. We want to learn and to love, to become whole, and the thing that stands most squarely in the way of that is fear.

I've chosen to talk about this in the context of "The new" for a couple of reasons. Fear is always of the future; never of the past, though the past haunts us; never of the present, though we have a devil of a time staying in the present. The new is the promise, the hope, the opportunity we are constantly moving into, moment by moment, as we live out our lives. I think it's important to exist in the present, yet be open to the fact that we're constantly moving into the future. Perls calls this a dilemma: "I say it's not possible to live in the here and now and yet nothing exists except the here and now." In *Gestalt Therapy Verbatim* he asks:

> How do we resolve this dilemma? What is buried in the word *now?* How come it takes years and years to understand a simple word like the word *now?* If I play a phonograph record, the sound of the record appears when the record and the needle touch each other, where they make contact. There is no sound of the before, there is no sound of the afterwards. If I stop the phonograph record, then the needle is still in contact with the record, but there is no music, because there is the absolute *now.* If you would blot out the past, or the anticipation of themes three minutes from now, you could not understand listening to that record you are now playing. But if you blot out the now, nothing will come through. So again, whether we remember or whether we anticipate, we do it *here and now.*[2]

[2] Fritz Perls, *Gestalt Therapy Verbatim* (Moab, Utah: Real People Press, 1969), p. 41.

We carry our past with us, often as excess baggage, into the now. We predict what our future will be, at the expense of *now*.

I think our concept of time has a lot to do with this. We invented the way we measure and think about time; why can't we invent other ways? In one moment of extreme clarity and profundity, I did just that and would like to share it with you. I had a picture of myself walking through a tunnel that was round and just barely bigger than I was, about 7 feet in diameter. Inside the tunnel, stretched all the way across and around the inside circumference, were thin, transparent plastic sheets and they were placed one after the other about an inch apart. As I walked I broke through the plastic sheets in succession. The sheets, or discs, which were a rosy red, represent increments of time. They could each represent a second, a microsecond, or a century—it doesn't matter. The tunnel is time, the discs an increment of my time and as I walk I am in the present, in some disc I am breaking; and in the future, stretching some disc to the breaking point with my foot or hand. The important difference, for me, in my "new time" is that time is stationary. It is standing still and I am moving.

The way we think about time is reflected in sayings like "My, how time flies." "Time passes you by." "Time waits for no man." I picture this man standing still with clocks and calendars whisking by him in a stiff wind, helpless to stop time from rushing on.

Another analogy comes to mind. The way most of us look at time is as if we were a rock in the middle of a river and the river—time—washed by us with hardly any regard for our existence. The way I am looking at time now is to say that I am the river moving on at my own pace, and time is the river bank.

What is this besides perhaps a funny mental exercise? This new way of thinking about time does several things for me. It takes some pressure off. It gives me a different sense of my movement in the world; I am moving ahead, making choices, breaking those discs that are my future. It gives me more responsibility and more power. It makes me feel as if I move at a pace that is more my own and am not so subject to tides and pulls of events around me.

When I am afraid, it is clear that is *my* fear; what I am

afraid of is beyond that next plastic sheet; and I can move to it. My fears have little to do with my fate being in the hands of others; I am more aware of my own choices and my willingness to move ahead when and how I want to. It means to me that I am moving into the future as I am in the present and as I am in the past. The new does not happen to me, assault me, from the outside alone. It is within me as well, waiting for me to discover and acknowledge it. There are parts of ourselves that we have not yet found, perhaps that we are afraid to explore. There are also parts of ourselves we must let go of, if new parts are to be born, if growth is to occur.

David Cole Gordon talked about this in relation to our fear of death:

> If we have associated life with both soul and self—and if we have been taught that, even if we gain the entire world, it is vain and empty because we lose our self or our soul—should we not dread its loss? When we think of our self, we think of it in terms of its being a conglomerate which is our essence; it is therefore natural to fear its loss. What could be more reasonable than to fear the loss of the self which we regard as a combination of our mind, our body, and everything that makes us unique?
>
> There are, of course, many social selves. . . . We are afraid most of all to lose the self that we are currently most identified with; we regard this self as our permanent self. Even though it is evident that our permanent self is subject to change, we tend to regard our present social self as permanent and to forget the many selves we have discarded and others that are likely to be born or created in the future. In short, what most of us regard as our self is nothing permanent, but is merely a constellation of changing thoughts orbiting around a physical body and relating to a certain number of people with whom we are in contact and involved with in certain activities.[3]

Again a paradox presents itself. If I am afraid of losing myself, I will lose myself. If I refuse to move into the active discovery of new parts of myself, out of a fear of loss of that "conglomerate self," or of losing old parts, I will stay in one

---

[3] David Cole Gordon, *Overcoming the Fear of Death* (New York: Macmillan Company, 1970). Copyright © 1969 by David Cole Gordon; reprinted by permission of Harold Matson Co., Inc.

place; I will stagnate. I will hold onto old behaviors that are inappropriate and/or harmful. Therefore I will lose the self I am becoming. I will stop growing. When I stop growing, or learning, I stop nourishing the me that gives and replenishes; I begin to lose my willingness to love.

Fantasies are one of the most important ways we preview new parts of ourselves. A fantasy or a dream can be an unfilled wish. It can be a kind of portrait we paint for ourselves of the future and we can almost get a feeling of what it would be like to be there. The more we can get in touch with our fantasies and dreams, the closer we can come to exploring what some of our frontiers are. Our fantasies also tell us what some of our needs are.

Several years ago I worked for the University of California in an office, in an office building, with lots of other people who came to work every morning at the same time and went home every night at the same time. I began to feel constrained by schedules, demands, and expectations of the university and those around me and I began to fantasize myself in an office at home. No schedule, no demands but my own, no pressures except those I agreed to. I had this picture of myself at my own desk, plunking away at my old Underwood, supporting myself as a free-lance writer. That fantasy got stronger and more frequent until I did something about it. It was my own message to myself as to what my next area of growth was; it was a picture I was painting for myself, a picture that was alluring and frightening at the same time. Could I make it on my own? What about my alimony and child support payments, not to mention rent, and food, and medical bills (without hospitalization)? Would I maintain the discipline that it takes to work on my own, day after day, with no one pushing? I probably couldn't get my job back.

But oh, the freedom, the luxurious freedom. I eased out. I dropped down to half-time for two years before I finally quit altogether. Today I'm plunking away at my old Underwood looking out the window of my home at the Pacific Ocean. The fears I had were all real, but not insurmountable. The fantasy picture I had is not completely filled in the way I thought it would be, but it's a lot closer to what I want than what I had.

I don't think this is any great tale of courage, but it is an example of a new part of myself coming up that I was willing to face and to act on. For me it has the feeling of a drive, a moving onward to fulfillment. Our fantasies or dreams can be directional signs, as encircled with fear as they may be; in fact, the more fear they hold for us, the more we may want them.

I want to relate this to creativity, because I have some ideals about the creative person that have to do with personal power, the new, and self-actualization. I think that the courage to create the new is one of the most important tasks we face, as individuals and as a society. It is what lifts us above the realm of other animals. It is man's purview to inaugurate rather than just continue and at this point in our history it seems imperative that we have the courage to create new structures, new forms, new social ways of being, new persons for the rapidly changing world we live in.

Rollo May calls this creative courage the willingness "to meet the anxiety of nothingness." To walk through this anxiety into the new, knowing that you may be wrong, is the key to our individual progress and our social progress together. It is the rarest kind of courage. Mary Caroline Richards, in her book *The Crossing Point*, talks about what this courage means to her and relates it to the process of making and firing ceramics:

> To transform our raw shapes into forms with deeper color and firmer use, we surrender them to the fire. Otherwise, they can be charming, exciting, fun, good—but they (we) cannot be fulfilled as vessels of life without the fire. We know this as a wisdom, but we have to find our way into it as a living experience. We have to discover what fire is—what heat is; if we want to change, we have to undertake it. We have to undergo the unknown. We cannot pull back and say No, I can't, I'm afraid. As potters we all know the feeling of risk and hope and anxiety when we put a pot in the kiln and never know exactly how it will come out—and we have worked hard on it. Of course we are afraid. But are we not afraid anyway—afraid of war, of the bomb, of death? Is it less fearful to die in a war than go through the ordeals of self-creation?
>
> Yes, of course, it is—it is less fearful to be a passive victim of a stronger force than it is to undergo inner loss and indeed a kind of inner death which precedes the birth of new capacities. Because the tender fragile trusting raw clay shape is gone forever once it is

submitted to the fire. We have to be willing to sacrifice it to the next level of maturity.[4]

Inner loss, inner death—those are frightening things to contemplate, but they must precede the birth of the new in us. It is not that fear is unappropriate or unnatural; it is very appropriate; it is the tension and the excitement and the signal that we are onto something, that some barrier is about to be broken, some threshold passed over. Without our fear we are foolish, but with a courage that is sensitive and unified we can enter into a collaboration with the blossoming new forms of ourselves and of the relationships we make. We cannot compare the new to the old at these moments but must face it squarely as it is.

One way I think about creativity is to say it's the externalization of internal excitation; at least that's the funny way I say it. It means that one way to create is to bring outside yourself the fantasies, dreams, myths, anger, love, fear that is going on inside; bring it out and act it out in such a way that it has a chance to be understood by others. As you bring it out and acknowledge it, it will return a gift to you; it will give you a new image, a new reflection of your self on your journey to self-knowledge.

This creative act, this exploration into the new, can be a breaking out of apathy, a rage against conformity and stagnation, a lunge out of depression or a bringing of unity to chaos. It can mean these things in personal terms or social terms. In creating, the individual is often acting against social norms or the status quo, which makes the act even more fearful and perhaps even more important. For this exploration of the new is vital to the social organism as well as the individual organism; as we ourselves hesitate from moving into new and frightening parts of ourselves we are, in a way, depriving our community of change and growth. It is likely that as I discover and explore some previously foreboding facet of my own personality, its expression will find some commonality in my peers.

Artists are the most ready example of this kind of process. A

---

[4] Copyright © 1966 by Mary Caroline Richards. Reprinted from *The Crossing Point*, by Mary Caroline Richards, by permission of Wesleyan University Press, p. 21.

community depends on its artists—though the dependency is not conscious in most cases—to be its conscience and to lead it into explorations of new life themes. Artists who are most responsive to themselves often find themselves on the "cutting edge" of the community or society they belong to and often find themselves controversial because they express values in conflict with many of the members of the community.

Painters, dramatists, sculptors, song-writers, poets, and novelists often raise strong feelings in a community not because they objectively stand off and assess a norm or look for a theme that "needs" exploring, but because they are delving into the most private and personal parts of themselves and their reactions to the world. We call their art "good" when that personal expression strikes a responsive chord in a large number of others; their personal truth is a statement we can adopt.

Others, of course, can make the same kind of social expression based on personal feelings and personal searches—scientists, doctors, social planners, lawyers. In each case as they act on this search, by transplanting a human heart for the first time or daring to introduce a liberalized abortion law, the important thing is not that their expression meets common agreement but that the issue is raised for public discussion. This constant raising of issues for decision making is essential to a healthy society and it springs from individuals who are willing to risk a public expression of a personal point of view. Looked at in this light, fear is not only a roadblock to our own personal growth but is a stagnation of social progress.

The fear that keeps us from venturing into the new and changing parts of ourselves—and only we know what those areas are—will often surprise us in finding commonality in our friends or in a larger community. Again, the first important step in that process is the willingness to be aware of who we are.

Sex is an area of ourselves and of our culture that provides a good example. We have seen in previous chapters how much of their sexual lives people are afraid of and we all know from either our own experiences or those of friends how laden with fear and guilt sex is for many of us. Healthy, open sexual expression has been repressed in most of us. Because we remain ignorant of a large area of ourselves and because we have been subject to punishment, ridicule, or rejection because of our sexual feelings, we are afraid of ourselves. We are afraid to give sexual pleasures to ourselves, we are afraid to openly desire someone, to give our sexual feelings full expression, and we are afraid of the "forbidden" fantasies that whirl through our minds in dreams or quiet daytime hours alone. It is this repression-fed fear that allows our sexual feelings to control us, in a bad way, and allows others in our capitalistic society to exploit those with no outlet for normal sexual desires.

For some of us, then, to explore the new might mean to be aware of, talk about, or act out a part of our own sexuality that we have been afraid to acknowledge or express. To rummage around in that tiny little nook that is inside us, to nurture it and bring it into the light, is one step toward developing our wholeness and unity. Our fear is what keeps us from it, from ourselves, but at the same time our fear is the label that lets us know "here is part of myself I need to know more about."

This movement into our fear and the expression of that process is not only a courageous and, in my view, a creative act, but is a move toward personal power and freedom as well. I'd like to say something about power and freedom. Fear, anxiety, confusion, depression—all these have a way of paralyzing us; another way of saying that is they take away our power and leave us in a kind of limbo or suspended state.

When Mary Caroline Richards wrote about going into the new, of collaborating with new forms, even though we are afraid, she added:

> Overcoming fear with a sensitive courage gives us two hands. We do not see well with one eye, we do not handle things well with one hand. It takes two.[5]

Henry Miller, in *The Wisdom of the Heart*, comes at the same idea from a slightly different direction:

> Everywhere we see life being lived vicariously. And yet life is everywhere and at all times for any and everybody is simple, startlingly simple. We live on the edge of the miraculous every minute of our lives. The miracle is in us, and it blossoms forth the

[5] Ibid., p. 75.

moment we lay ourselves open to it. The miracle of miracles is the stubbornness with which men refuse to open themselves up. Our whole life seems to be nothing but a frantic effort to evade that which is constantly within our grasp. This which is the very reverse of the miraculous is nothing else but FEAR. Man has no other real enemy than this which he carries within him. Somewhere a French poet has written: "No daring is fatal." Provided, he should have added, that one is unified. Divided, everything is fatal and leads to catastrophe. . . . The whole man must be there, ready at all times to act (or not to act), to move with the certitude of a sleepwalker, to dare anything because he is convinced that life is now, this very moment, and that it is inexhaustible and unknowable.[6]

I find that an elegant statement, one of my favorite quotes. In the final sentence I think Miller is talking about a personal power based on knowing what we want and need, and acting on it, *now*. Both writers are urging us to use our ears and eyes and hands, our sensitivities, and act out of what we sense is best for us. Inherent in those statements, as I read them, is a trust that we each know somewhere inside what it is that we need and want, if we can only listen and act with trust in ourselves.

Let me come at it from yet another angle. Three years ago, in the preparation of an earlier book called *How Do You Feel?* I wrote this about my own anxiety:

> I'm anxious today. I see myself flit from small task to small task, not pausing long enough to get settled at any one thing. The pleasant warmth of the day and the calm way others seem around me seems only to accentuate my nervousness. Occasionally, I catch myself with a wrinkled brow and tight eyes, my shoulders sneaking in toward my neck—how can I head that off?
>
> I prepare curt, testy replies to imagined encounters with others in the house; there seems to be a quick, hard-shelled defense right at the surface. What is under that? What am I worried about defending? I have brought out—superficially—some "borderline" worries; money, a general aimlessness. But deeper than that I know I am worried about Betsy coming back. A separation of five months, a trip for her of more than a month

---

[6] Henry Miller, *The Wisdom of the Heart.* Copyright 1941 by New Directions Publishing Corporation. Reprinted by permission of New Directions Publishing Corporation.

and now two days together before she leaves again. I'm sweating. I don't know what to expect. I don't want to expect too much and pressure us both so we can't relax with each other. And trying to expect little or nothing seems to make me apathetic. The waiting! That's what screws me up.

I seem to be suspended in some kind of powerless limbo, waiting for her to make up her mind, waiting for her to do something to respond to. And I begin to think that if I can stop waiting, take some power of my own, take responsibility only for myself and *do* what it is I want to, I will be less anxious. That is, my anxiety has to do with fearing the unknown and, in this situation, subtly giving up most of the power over what happens to Betsy.

The unknown is still there. But I will surely feel better about it if I can go into this in touch with my own needs and feelings and not so worried about and dependent on her actions or what will go on between us.[7]

The core of that statement means very much to me today. I will catch myself and others sitting in some kind of anxious limbo, waiting for someone else—a person or an institution—to act. The more I do that, the more I live in fear, for I am giving up the power of making choices about my life to others. As I do that I get further into a web of anxiety, resentment, blame, and dependency. When I can stop and take account of what my needs are and act on those feelings, I am pulling myself out of my own anxiousness into a place of personal power. It is not that I will not be afraid; I may be even more afraid when I begin to make decisions and take action, but I will not let the fear hold me down. I will act *with* fear, with the tension and energy it brings rather than sit and hold it inside, watching the world go by.

It is easy to forget that fear has a lot of energy behind it. Our challenge is to take that energy and act on it, not in random, erratic ways, directed at the wrong people or things, but to turn it around on its source; use the tension fear gives you to explore the very thing you're afraid of. Our fear can be, if we change our way of looking at it, a signal light, a gate, an opportunity to expand and strengthen ourselves.

[7] John T. Wood, *How Do You Feel? A Guide to Your Emotions* (Englewood Cliffs, N.J.: Prentice-Hall, Inc., 1974), p. 40.

Rainer Maria Rilke, the German poet, says this in such a beautiful way in a small volume of *Letters to a Young Poet*:

> We have no reason to mistrust our world, for it is not against us. Has it terrors, they are *our* terrors; has it abysses, those abysses belong to us; are dangers at hand, we must try to love them. And if only we arrange our life according to that principle which counsels us that we must always hold to the difficult, then that which now still seems to us the most alien will become what we most trust and find most faithful. How should we be able to forget those ancient myths that are at the beginning of all peoples, the myths about dragons that at the last moment turn into princesses; perhaps all the dragons of our lives are princesses who are only waiting to see us once beautiful and brave. Perhaps everything terrible is in its deepest being something helpless that wants help from us.[8]

Suppose all our dragons are princesses in disguise? Think of all the dragons in your life. Imagine them all as opportunities, invitations even, to gain a new part of your self, to absorb power that you've lost, to fill up an empty void.

The new frightens most of us. You will find a lot of company in being afraid of what is going to happen. What is harder to find are people (and perhaps the part of yourself) willing to move into the unknown, people who will embrace the things most all of us are afraid of in order to keep growing toward creativity, power, and one other very valuable thing, freedom.

As part of the research I did on fear, I interviewed a couple about the things they were afraid of. The woman started right out with:

> Usually the thing that scares me the most is the unknown. I am scared sometimes by things I know are going to happen, but the things I don't know about bring me the most anxiety and the most physical reactions.

---

[8] Reprinted from *Letters to a Young Poet* by Rainer Maria Rilke. Translation by M. D. Herter Norton. By permission of W. W. Norton & Company, Inc., and Hogarth Press, Ltd., London. Copyright 1934 by W. W. Norton & Company, Inc. Copyright renewed 1962 by M. D. Herter Norton. Revised edition copyright 1954 by W. W. Norton & Company, Inc.

She went on into two important areas, the fears of her own growth, of what she was going to change into as she helped herself and learned from others. She also talked about her fears of what her husband would grow into as he changed.

"I sometimes worry about his growth," she said. "He goes after what he wants and he becomes different and I get afraid of what that will do to our relationship and to me." That scared her. Her own growth, her husband's, their relationship—but did it paralyze her? Not as I experienced her. She was too valuable to herself and she valued her husband and their marriage too much to allow herself to be stuck in that glue of anxiety she sensed, all too much, in evidence. Later in the interview she said:

> One of the things I'd like to be able to do is be quicker to realize what I'm feeling is fear. Obviously I can't deal with it until I know it. A lot of times it takes me a while to say to myself "Hey, I'm scared." I might avoid doing something or tell myself I can't do it, all the while not admitting that I'm afraid to do it.
>
> The way I want to deal with fear is not to avoid what I'm afraid of. I can't deal with it until I face it. That's the only way I can conquer it, to walk into it, whatever it is.

Where did that "walking into it" get her? What's the reward for facing down the dragons of our lives? Her husband answered:

> Most every time I test my freedom, I find that the boundary is mine, the restriction is my own and not one that is in my environment or that someone else is putting on me. That knowledge, in a sense, makes me free and my freedom is limited only by my fear of risking. My freedom is change; I can't do what I want to do and have things stay the same.
>
> The most important thing I've learned about my freedom is learning where my nonfreedom lies. I think I'm a very fortunate man and in many ways a great deal freer than many people I know. For the most part, my freedom lies in me. The opposite of my freedom is fear and I maintain that nonfreedom by failing to challenge my fear.

Every move we make in freedom is a movement into the new, the unknown. Every move we make toward the things we are afraid of is a move toward wholeness, unity, joy. The arenas may be different for each of us, but each of us—remember, each of us—faces the uniquely human frontier that is within, the urge to become more than we are. When that ceases, we begin to die.

For that ceaseless, complicated, and fearful journey there are no road maps and there are few rules or guidelines to follow. We are explorers. The territories are not the oceans, the mountain ranges, or outer space. Our frontiers are within ourselves as individuals and in the relationships we build with one another. That journey, toward love, is filled with risks and challenges; it is natural to be afraid. But the discoveries we make along the way, of creativity, freedom, potency, and intimacy help us know that we can't turn back.

Picking up this book, you might have thought the message might have been "Don't be Afraid." It is not. Be afraid. Court your fear as you would a lover. Treat her as a princess who is hiding behind the mask of a dragon.

A beginning, hopefully...

Index

Advertising, 103
Allen, George, 123
Alsop, Stewart, 68
Anatomy of Courage (Lord Moran), 68–69
Anger, 22–23
    fear of, 146–47
    relationship of fear to, 46–50
Anxiety, 32–40, 44–46
Aronson, Marvin L., 42–44
Art of Growing, The (Nixon), 37–39
Asner, Ed, 13
Authority figures, 9–11, 48, 49
Auw, Andre, 52–53

Baker, Howard, 14
Baldwin, James, 12
Behavior therapy, 25–26, 141, 143–48

Biological Boundaries of Learning, The (Seligman and Hager), 26
Birney, Robert, 81, 83
Birth, 3–4
Bodily responses to fear, 22–23
Bridges, Lloyd, 13
Browne, Sir Thomas, 134
Burdick, Harvey, 81, 83

Center for Policy Research, 9
Children
    dependence of, 12, 51
    fears of, 5–7, 84–85
    phobias, 41, 42
    sexuality, 126
Client-centered therapy, 141, 149–51, 155
Comfort, Alex, 128–30

Conquest of Fear (King), 4–5
Control, 29, 85, 122–25
Coping response, 30
Creativity, 70–71, 107, 165–67
Crimes, 8–9, 28, 107
Cronkite, Walter, 100
Crossing Point, The (Richards), 165–66, 168
cummings, e. e., 108

Daddy's Girl (Wells), 49, 142–43
Davies, Peter, 96
Death, fear of, 18–20, 31, 68, 124, 133–39, 163
Deification, 103–4
Dependency, relationship of fear to, 12, 50–52
Desire, fear and, 113–21, 137
Devil, belief in the, 9
Differentness, 88, 108
Disagreement, 88
Displacement, 43

Encounter groups, 154
Evolutionary basis of fears, 26–27

Failure, fear of, 31, 50, 51–52, 80–84, 89, 116, 118–19
Fantasies, 43, 164–65
Fast, Julius, 130
Fear of Failure (Birney, Burdick, and Teevan), 81, 83
Fire Next Time, The (Baldwin), 12
Football, 96–97
Ford, Gerald, 95–96, 98
Francis, Anne, 13
Freedom, 171–72
Freud, Sigmund, 34, 40, 151
Freudian therapy, 148
Frustration, relationship of fear to, 50

Gaynor, Mitzi, 13
Gestalt therapy, 141, 151
Gestalt Therapy Verbatim (Perls), 35, 151–52, 161

God, fear of, 4, 9
Goethe, Johann Wolfgang von, 138
Gordon, David Cole, 10, 20, 134–37, 163
Gornick, Vivian, 113
Gould, Roger, 160
Guilt, relationship of fear to, 52–53

Hager, Joanne, 26
Hall, Stanley, 6
Haver, June, 13
Hearts and Minds (movie), 96
Hemingway, Ernest, 140
Hesse, Hermann, 70–71
How Do You Feel? A Guide to Your Emotions (Wood), 78–79, 169–70
How to Overcome Your Fear of Flying (Aronson), 42

Implosion therapy, 141, 148–49, 156
Impotence, fear of, 129–31
Insecurity, relationship of fear to, 53–55, 87
Intimacy, 17–19, 74–89
Irrational conscience, 42–43

John, St., 76
Johnson, Virginia, 129, 130
Joy of Sex, The (Comfort), 128–30

Keyes, Ralph, 19
King, Basil, 4–5
Kinsey, Alfred C., 129, 130
Klein, Carole, 7

Lester, Richard, 13
Letters to a Young Poet (Rilke), 171
Littlefair, Duncan, 95–96
Loneliness, fear of, 17, 31
Loss of control, fear of, 109, 115, 123, 132

McGovern, George, 94
"Macho" attitude, 96, 97
McLuhan, Marshall, 102
McNamara, Robert, 97

Man Against Himself (Menninger), 127
Manipulation, 85
Maslow, Abraham, 7
Masters, William, 129, 130
May, Rollo, 35–36, 94, 165
Maya, 153, 157
Media, 98–103
Meir, Golda, 13–14
Menninger, Karl, 127
Miller, Henry, 66, 168–69
Miller, Neal, 61–62
Moran, Lord, 68–69
Motion picture industry, 101

Narcissus and Goldmund (Hesse), 70–71
Needs, hierarchy of, 7
Newspapers, 98–103
Nitze, Paul, 97
Nixon, Richard, 94, 97, 98, 103
Nixon, Robert, 37–39
Notes to Myself (Prather), 66

Orgasm, 132–33, 137
Outsiders, fear of, 91, 93, 94, 95, 98
Overcoming the Fear of Death (Gordon), 10, 134–37

Paton, Alan, 70, 105–6
Pentagon Papers, 96, 97
Perls, Fritz, 35, 53, 161
Person-centered therapy, *see* Client-centered therapy
Phobias, 32, 33, 40–44
Political leaders, 10–11, 94–98
Politics, fear and, 94–98
Possessiveness, 119
Powerlessness, sense of, 94, 95, 154
Prather, Hugh, 66, 71
Predictability, 28–30
Punishment, fear of, 31, 48, 61–65, 83, 126–28

Race relations, 12, 92–94, 105–6
Rand, Peter, 95–96
Reich, Wilhelm, 133

Reidy, Jeanne, 35
Rejection, fear of, 31, 109, 115, 116, 119–20
Religion, 9–10
Resentment, 53
Responsibility, 121, 154–55
Richards, Mary Caroline, 165–66, 168
Rilke, Rainer Maria, 171
Risk of Loving, The (Simons and Reidy), 35
Rogers, Carl, 150–51
Rosenberg, Jack Lee, 132–33
Ross, Chris, 67–68
Rush, Benjamin, 5

Scarf, Maggie, 26, 27
School integration, 92–94
Schuller, Robert, 80
Schwartz, Robert, 93
Self-actualization, 7, 160
Self-image, 78–79, 81, 125–26
Self-Love: The Dynamic Force of Success (Schuller), 80
Self-respect, 68–69
Seligman, Martin, 26–27, 29
Sexual fears, 16–17, 43, 84, 124–33, 138, 167–68
Smith, Huston, 153
Socrates, 134
Speaking in public, fear of, 11
Stampfl, Thomas G., 148–49
Stay of Execution: A Sort of Memoir (Alsop), 68
Sullivan, Harry Stack, 35
Surrender, 17, 19, 20, 123–25, 132, 138
Systematic desensitization, 144, 156

Teevan, Richard, 81, 83
Television, 98–103
Three Pillars of Zen, The (Smith), 153
Time, concept of, 135, 162
Time magazine, 8–9
Total Orgasm (Rosenberg), 132–33
Trust, 88, 138, 169

Unification experience, 136–39
Unknown, fear of the, 38–39, 135, 161–72
Unpredictability, 28–30
Urban living, 8–9

Valentine, C. W., 26
Vascancellos, John, 7–8
Vietnam War, 96, 97, 123
Voting, 94–95
Vulnerability, 84

Waggoner, Lyle, 13
Walker, Clint, 13
Washington Post, 92
Watchtower, 8, 9

Watson, John B., 25
We, the Lonely People (Keyes), 19
Weiss, Jay, 30
Well, Judith, 49, 142–43
What You Should Know About Human Sexual Response (Fast), 130
Wisdom of the Heart, The (Miller), 66, 168–69
Wolves, 104
Women's liberation, 75

Young, Paul Thomas, 34

Zane, Manuel, 145
Zen, 153, 157